AQA History

AS
Unit 2

The ... lin's
Lead...ip in the USSR,
1924–1941

Exclusively endorsed by AQA

John Laver

Series editor
Sally Waller

...ornes

Published in 2008 by:
Nelson Thornes Ltd
Delta Place
27 Bath Road
CHELTENHAM
GL53 7TH
United Kingdom

08 09 10 11 12 / 10 9 8 7 6 5 4 3 2 1

A catalogue record for this book is available from the British Library

978-0-7487-8267-3

Illustrations by David Russell Illustration

Page make-up by Thomson Digital

Printed in Great Britain by Scotprint

Contents

AQA introduction

Nelson Thornes and AQA

Nelson Thornes has worked in collaboration with AQA to ensure that this book offers you the best support for your AS or A level course and helps you to prepare for your exams. The partnership means that you can be confident that the range of learning, teaching and assessment practice materials has been checked by the senior examining team at AQA before formal approval, and is closely matched to the requirements of your specification.

Blended learning

This book forms a blend with electronic resources: this means that links between topics and activities between the book and the electronic resources help you to work in the way that best suits you, and enable extra support to be provided online. For example, you can test yourself online and feedback from the test will direct you back to the relevant parts of the book.

Electronic resources are available in a simple-to-use online platform called Nelson Thornes learning space. If your school or college has a licence to use the service, you will be given a password through which you can access the materials through any internet connection.

Learning activity

These resources include a variety of interactive and non-interactive activities to support your learning.

Progress tracking

These resources include a variety of tests that you can use to check your knowledge on particular topics (Test yourself) and a range of resources that enable you to analyse and understand examination questions (On your marks…).

Research support

These resources include WebQuests, in which you are assigned a task and provided with a range of web links to use as source material for research.

Study skills

These resources support you to develop a skill that is key for your course, for example planning essays.

When you see an icon, go to Nelson Thornes learning space at www.nelsonthornes.com/aqagce, enter your access details and select your course. The materials are arranged in the same order as the topics in the book, so you can easily find the resources you need.

How to use this book

This book covers the specification for your course and is arranged in a sequence approved by AQA.

The features in this book include:

Timeline

Key events are outlined at the beginning of the book. The events are colour-coded so you can clearly see the categories of change.

Learning objectives

At the beginning of each section you will find a list of learning objectives that contain targets linked to the requirements of the specification.

Key chronology

A short list of dates usually with a focus on a specific event or legislation.

Key profile

The profile of a key person you should be aware of to fully understand the period in question.

Key term

A term that you will need to be able to define and understand.

Did you know?

Interesting information to bring the subject under discussion to life.

Exploring the detail

Information to put further context around the subject under discussion.

A closer look

An in-depth look at a theme, person or event to deepen your understanding. Activities around the extra information may be included.

Sources

Sources to reinforce topics or themes and may provide fact or opinion. They may be quotations from historical works, contemporaries of the period or photographs.

Cross-reference

Links to related content which may offer more detail on the subject in question.

Activity

Various activity types to provide you with different challenges and opportunities to demonstrate both the content and skills you are learning. Some can be worked on individually, some as part of group work and some are designed to specifically "stretch and challenge".

Question

Questions to prompt further discussion on the topic under consideration and are an aid to revision.

Summary questions

Summary questions at the end of each chapter to test your knowledge and allow you to demonstrate your understanding.

AQA Examiner's tip

Hints from AQA examiners to help you with your study and to prepare for your exam.

AQA Examination-style questions

Questions at the end of each section in the style that you can expect in your exam.

Learning outcomes

Learning outcomes at the end of each section remind you what you should know having completed the chapters in that section.

Web links in the book

Because Nelson Thornes is not responsible for third party content online, there may be some changes to this material that are beyond our control. In order for us to ensure that the links referred to in the book are as up-to-date and stable as possible, the web sites provided are usually homepages with supporting instructions on how to reach the relevant pages if necessary.

Please let us know at **webadmin@nelsonthornes.com** if you find a link that doesn't work and we will do our best to correct this at reprint, or to list an alternative site.

Introduction to the History series

When Bruce Bogtrotter in Roald Dahl's *Matilda* was challenged to eat a huge chocolate cake, he just opened his mouth and ploughed in, taking bite after bite and lump after lump until the cake was gone and he was feeling decidedly sick. The picture is not dissimilar to that of some A level history students. They are attracted to history because of its inherent appeal but, when faced with a bulging file and a forthcoming examination, their enjoyment evaporates. They try desperately to cram their brains with an assortment of random facts and subsequently prove unable to control the outpouring of their ill-digested material in the examination.

The books in this series are designed to help students and teachers avoid this feeling of overload and examination panic by breaking down the AQA history specification in such a way that it is easily absorbed. Above all, they are designed to retain and promote students' enthusiasm for history by avoiding a dreary rehash of dates and events. Each book is divided into sections, closely matched to those given in the specification, and the content is further broken down into chapters that present the historical material in a lively and attractive form, offering guidance on the key terms, events and issues, and blending thought-provoking activities and questions in a way designed to advance students' understanding. By encouraging students to think for themselves and to share their ideas with others, as well as helping them to develop the knowledge and skills they will need to pass their examination, this book should ensure that students' learning remains a pleasure rather than an endurance test.

To make the most of what this book provides, students will need to develop efficient study skills from the start and it is worth spending some time considering what these involve:

- Good organisation of material in a subject-specific file. Organised notes help develop an organised brain and sensible filing ensures time is not wasted hunting for misplaced material. This book uses cross-references to indicate where material in one chapter has relevance to material in another. Students are advised to adopt the same technique.

- A sensible approach to note-making. Students are often too ready to copy large chunks of material from printed books or to download sheaves of printouts from the internet. This series is designed to encourage students to think about the notes they collect and to undertake research with a particular purpose in mind. The activities encourage students to pick out information that is relevant to the issue being addressed and to avoid making notes on material that is not properly understood.

- Taking time to think, which is by far the most important component of study. By encouraging students to think before they write or speak, be it for a written answer, presentation or class debate, students should learn to form opinions and make judgements based on the accumulation of evidence. These are the skills that the examiner will be looking for in the final examination. The beauty of history is that there is rarely a right or wrong answer so, with sufficient evidence, one student's view will count for as much as the next.

Unit 2

Unit 2 promotes the study of significant periods of history in depth. Although the span of years may appear short, the chosen topics are centred on periods of change that raise specific historical issues and they therefore provide an opportunity for students to study in some depth the interrelationships between ideas, individuals, circumstances and other factors that lead to major developments. Appreciating the dynamics of change, and balancing the degree of change against elements of continuity, make for a fascinating and worthwhile study. Students are also required to analyse consequences and draw conclusions about the issues these studies raise. Such themes are, of course, relevant to an understanding of the present and, through such an historical investigation, students will be guided towards a greater appreciation of the world around them today, as well as develop their understanding of the past.

Unit 2 is tested by a 1 hour 30 minute paper containing three questions. The first question is compulsory and based on sources, while the remaining two, of which students will need to choose one, are two-part questions as described in Table 1. Plentiful sources are included throughout this book to give students some familiarity with contemporary and historiographical material, and activities and suggestions are provided to enable students to develop the required examination skills. Students should familiarise themselves with the question breakdown, additional hints and marking criteria given below before attempting any of the practice examination-style questions at the end of each section.

Answers will be marked according to a scheme based on 'levels of response'. This means that the answer will be assessed according to which level best matches the historical skills displayed, taking both knowledge and understanding into account. All students should have a copy of these criteria and need to use them wisely.

Table 1 *Unit 2: style of questions and marks available*

Unit 2	Question	Marks	Question type	Question stem	Hints for students
Question 1 based on three sources of c.300 – 350 words in total	(a)	12	This question involves the comparison of two sources	Explain how far the views in Source B differ from those in Source A in relation to…	Take pains to avoid simply writing out what each source says with limited direct comment. Instead, you should try to find two or three points of comparison and illustrate these with reference to the sources. You should also look for any underlying similarities. In your conclusion, you will need to make it clear exactly 'how far' the views differ
Question 1	(b)	24	This requires use of the sources and own knowledge and asks for an explanation that shows awareness that issues and events can provoke differing views and explanations	How far… How important was… How successful…	This answer needs to be planned as you will need to develop an argument in your answer and show balanced judgement. Try to set out your argument in the introduction and, as you develop your ideas through your paragraphs, support your opinions with detailed evidence. Your conclusion should flow naturally and provide supported judgement. The sources should be used as 'evidence' throughout your answer. Do ensure you refer to them all
Question 2 and 3	(a)	12	This question is focused on a narrow issue within the period studied and requires an explanation	Explain why…	Make sure you explain 'why', not 'how', and try to order your answer in a way that shows you understand the inter-linkage of factors and which are the most important. You should try to reach an overall judgement/conclusion
Question 2 and 3	(b)	24	This question is broader and asks for analysis and explanation with appropriate judgement. The question requires an awareness of debate over issues	A quotation in the form of a judgement on a key development or issue will be given and candidates asked: Explain why you agree or disagree with this view (of… in the years…)	This answer needs to be planned as you will need to show balanced judgement. Try to think of points that agree and disagree and decide which way you will argue. Set out your argument in the introduction and support it through your paragraphs, giving the alternative picture too but showing why your view is the more convincing. Your conclusion should flow naturally from what you have written

Marking criteria

Question 1(a)

Level 1 Answers either briefly paraphrase/describe the content of the two sources or identify simple comparison(s) between the sources. Skills of written communication will be weak. *(0–2 marks)*

Level 2 Responses will compare the views expressed in the two sources and identify some differences and/or similarities. There may be some limited own knowledge. Answers will be coherent but weakly expressed. *(3–6 marks)*

Level 3 Responses will compare the views expressed in the two sources, identifying differences **and** similarities and using own knowledge to explain and evaluate these. Answers will, for the most part, be clearly expressed. *(7–9 marks)*

Level 4 Responses will make a developed comparison between the views expressed in the two sources **and** own knowledge will apply to evaluate and to demonstrate a good contextual understanding. Answers will, for the most part, show good skills of written communication. *(10–12 marks)*

Question 1(b)

Level 1 Answers may be based on sources or on own knowledge alone, or they may comprise an undeveloped mixture of the two. They may contain some descriptive material which is only loosely linked to the focus of the question or they may address only a part of the question. Alternatively, there may be some explicit comment with little, if any, appropriate support. Answers are likely to be generalised and assertive. There will be little, if any, awareness of differing historical interpretations. The response will be limited in development and skills of written communication will be weak. *(0–6 marks)*

Level 2 Answers may be based on sources or on own knowledge alone, or they may contain a mixture of the two. They may be almost entirely descriptive with few explicit links to the focus of the question. Alternatively, they may contain some explicit comment with relevant but limited support. They will display limited understanding of differing historical interpretations. Answers will be coherent but weakly expressed and/or poorly structured. *(7–11 marks)*

Level 3 Answers will show a developed understanding of the demands of the question using evidence from **both** the sources **and** own knowledge. They will provide some assessment backed by relevant and appropriately selected evidence, but they will lack depth and/or balance. There will be some understanding of varying historical interpretations. Answers will, for the most part, be clearly expressed and show some organisation in the presentation of material. *(12–16 marks)*

Level 4 Answers will show explicit understanding of the demands of the question. They will develop a balanced argument backed by a good range of appropriately selected evidence from the sources and own knowledge, and a good understanding of historical interpretations. Answers will, for the most part, show organisation and good skills of written communication. *(17–21 marks)*

Level 5 Answers will be well focused and closely argued. The arguments will be supported by precisely selected evidence from the sources and own knowledge, incorporating well-developed understanding of historical interpretations and debate. Answers will, for the most part, be carefully organised and fluently written, using appropriate vocabulary. *(22–24 marks)*

Question 2(a) and 3(a)

Level 1 Answers will contain either some descriptive material which is only loosely linked to the focus of the question or some explicit comment with little, if any, appropriate support. Answers are likely to be generalised and assertive. The response will be limited in development and skills of written communication will be weak. *(0–2 marks)*

Level 2 Answers will demonstrate some knowledge and understanding of the demands of the question. They will either be almost entirely descriptive with few explicit links to the question **or** they provide some explanations backed by evidence that is limited in range and/or depth. Answers will be coherent but weakly expressed and/or poorly structured. *(3–6 marks)*

Level 3 Answers will demonstrate good understanding of the demands of the question providing relevant explanations backed by appropriately selected information, although this may not be full or comprehensive. Answers will, for the most part, be clearly expressed and show some organisation in the presentation of material. *(7–9 marks)*

Level 4 Answers will be well focused, identifying a range of specific explanations backed by precise evidence and demonstrating good understanding of the connections and links between events/issues. Answers will, for the most part, be well written and organised. *(10–12 marks)*

Question 2(b) and 3(b)

Level 1 Answers may **either** contain some descriptive material which is only loosely linked to the focus of the question **or** they may address only a limited part of the period of the question. Alternatively, there may be some explicit comment with little, if any, appropriate support. Answers are likely to be generalised and assertive. There will be little, if any, awareness of different historical interpretations. The response will be limited in development and skills of written communication will be weak. *(0–6 marks)*

Level 2 Answers will show some understanding of the demands of the question. They will either be almost entirely descriptive with few explicit links to the question **or** they contain some explicit comment with relevant but limited support. They will display limited understanding of differing historical interpretations. Answers will be coherent but weakly expressed and/or poorly structured. *(7–11 marks)*

Level 3 Answers will show a developed understanding of the demands of the question. They will provide some assessment, backed by relevant and appropriately selected evidence, but they will lack depth and/or balance. There will be some understanding of varying historical interpretations. Answers will, for the most part, be clearly expressed and show some organisation in the presentation of material. *(12–16 marks)*

Level 4 Answers will show explicit understanding of the demands of the question. They will develop a balanced argument backed by a good range of appropriately selected evidence and a good understanding of historical interpretations. Answers will, for the most part, show organisation and good skills of written communication. *(17–21 marks)*

Level 5 Answers will be well focused and closely argued. The arguments will be supported by precisely selected evidence leading to a relevant conclusion/judgement, incorporating well-developed understanding of historical interpretations and debate. Answers will, for the most part, be carefully organised and fluently written, using appropriate vocabulary. *(22–24 marks)*

Introduction to this book

Key terms

Constituent Assembly: the parliament elected soon after the Bolshevik Revolution. The elections did not produce a Bolshevik majority and therefore Lenin immediately closed down the assembly, and the Bolsheviks ruled by force.

Mensheviks: the group of Social Democrats (SDP) that did not become part of Lenin's Bolshevik group when the SDP divided in 1903. The Mensheviks formed a separate party in August 1917 and did not take part in the October Revolution. The party was suppressed in 1922, although some members survived and were put on trial in 1930.

Socialist Revolutionaries: a radical party formed in the 1890s, and looking to the peasants as a revolutionary force. The party split, and Left SRs collaborated with the Bolsheviks in 1917. However, the party was effectively suppressed by the Bolsheviks by 1920.

Former Russian Empire: following the 1917 Revolution, the Bolsheviks inherited the vast imperial Russian Empire. The largest part was Russia, but the empire also included many other territories, including Muslim territories in Asia; the Ukraine; and territories in the South such as Georgia, which was Stalin's homeland. Although in theory all these territories were given independence, by the time of Lenin's death they had all been incorporated into the USSR (The Union of Soviet Socialist Republics), ruled from Moscow by the Communist Party.

The USSR at the time of Lenin's death in 1924

Lenin's death in 1924 came as a great shock to most Russians. He had, along with colleagues such as Leon Trotsky, led the October 1917 Revolution that brought the Bolsheviks to power in Petrograd and Moscow. Between 1917 and 1921, Lenin had presided over the creation of the new Soviet State at the same time as the Bolsheviks, or the Communists as they were increasingly known, fought a bitter civil war against their opponents. First they had to survive and then consolidate their power. However, soon after, when survival and peace seemed more certain in 1921, Lenin increasingly fell victim to bad health and gradually lost his grip on power, although he retained the respect of all his followers. Some time before his death, there were already moves amongst his leading colleagues to jockey for position in the Russia that would develop after Lenin's death. Stalin was already a prominent Bolshevik, although less in the public eye than more flamboyant colleagues like Trotsky. Stalin's great strength was his influence in the Communist Party organisation, which already dominated most aspects of Soviet life by the time of Lenin's death.

Creating the new Soviet State

Following the Bolshevik Revolution of 1917, Lenin's main priorities had been to make peace with Germany and to lead the new Bolshevik State through the desperate struggle for survival in the Civil War (1918–21). The Bolsheviks had to fight off many opponents such as:

- other left-wing revolutionary groups, which objected to the Bolshevik seizure of power and subsequent actions such as the closing down of the newly elected **Constituent Assembly** when it proved not to have a Bolshevik majority. Opposition groups included many **Mensheviks** and **Socialist Revolutionaries**.

- opponents to the right of the Bolsheviks, including people like landlords and businessmen who found their property confiscated and other rights taken from them in the name of the 'Russian people'

- former tsarist generals, who objected to Bolshevik actions such as signing the Treaty of Brest-Litovsk, which made large concessions to Germany in order to stop the German invasion

- some members of national groups within the **former Russian Empire**, seeking to establish their own breakaway states

- armies from 17 foreign nations, including Britain, the USA, France and Japan. These foreign governments had various motives, ranging from a desire to get Russia back into the war with Germany; to crush Communism, which they feared might provoke an international workers' revolution spreading to their own countries; to realising their own territorial ambitions. Their military efforts were on the whole half-hearted, mainly the result of exhaustion following several years of world war.

Besides outright opponents of the Bolsheviks, there were large numbers of Russians, including the bulk of the peasantry, who had no particular time for either side in the Civil War, but just wanted to get on with their own lives in peace. The peasants' concern was to scratch a living from the land, which in many cases they had seized for themselves during or just after the Revolution. The opponents of the Bolsheviks, collectively known as the Whites, had in common with each other only their hatred of the Bolsheviks. They were no match for the Red Army, skilfully and ruthlessly led by Lenin's right-hand man Leon Trotsky. The Bolsheviks also had major advantages such as control of the main industrial areas of Russia, unity under Lenin's leadership, and the psychological advantage of knowing that they had to fight with the utmost determination to avoid complete destruction.

During the Civil War, despite the desperate struggle for survival, the Bolsheviks attempted to create a new society. Radical policies were introduced. Land could no longer be bought, sold or rented, although since it could still be privately owned, this measure did not go as far as many Bolsheviks wanted, with their vision of a classless society in which everything was held in common. Other nationalities within the old Russian Empire were given the right of self-determination, meaning the right to govern themselves. In factories, workers' committees were given the right to supervise managers. Industry was nationalised in 1918. There was a range of social legislation: an eight-hour day for workers, legal equality for women, the introduction of civil marriage and divorce, the nationalisation of Church property and the abolition of titles and class distinctions.

These measures were regarded at the time as very adventurous, and downright dangerous by the governments of other world powers. At the same time as passing revolutionary decrees, the Bolsheviks were introducing a rigidly controlled and policed society that did not tolerate any alternative viewpoint:

■ Under the pressure of war and reflecting the previous history of the Bolsheviks as a tightly-knit, secretive, authoritarian-led party, local Bolshevik **Soviets** quickly lost their independence, and had to take orders from Moscow.

■ There was the ruthless use of terror against real or suspected opponents. The chief instrument of terror was the **Cheka**.

■ The inability of the Bolsheviks during the Civil War to feed the towns or Red Army adequately led to the application of **War Communism** in 1918. All economic activity was subordinated to the needs of winning the war. All industry was nationalised and there was forced requisitioning of food from the peasants, regardless of their own needs.

■ Other measures were taken to silence opposition, real or imagined, to the Bolsheviks. These included censorship of the press and attacks on religious beliefs. Propaganda was an important weapon of the government, backed up by force.

The context of Stalin's rise to power

The repressive measures were directly relevant to the later Stalinist period. The early Bolshevik State was born in violence and, to a large extent, maintained itself by violence, although there was also much idealism amongst young Communists. Many of the Communists and officials who implemented these measures went on to positions of influence in the next two decades, although eventually many of them were brutally eliminated by Stalin in the purges of the later 1930s. However, in the 1920s, these men brought their experience of revolution and war with them, and it made them quite prepared to act decisively and ruthlessly in the interests of the State even when the regime was more

■ **Key terms**

Soviets: the Russian word for 'council'. A revolutionary Soviet had been set up in St Petersburg during the 1905 Revolution, and reappeared after the 1917 February Revolution. Most of its members were elected by workers, soldiers or sailors.

Cheka: the All-Russian Extraordinary Commission for Combating Counter-revolution and Sabotage was led by a Polish aristocrat called Felix Dzerzhinsky. It had the power to investigate, arrest, interrogate, try and execute any opponents of the regime. The Cheka created the first Soviet labour camps and is estimated to have been responsible for up to 200,000 deaths. It was replaced by the GPU in 1922.

■ Cross-reference

For more information on the Cheka see page 97.

firmly established and there was peace in the USSR. The siege mentality created during the early years of struggle was always there just below the surface in the later 1920s and was resurrected even more strongly by Stalin during the 1930s. Stalin himself was one of the 'old warriors' who had learned how to survive through a mixture of hard work, cunning and ruthlessness in service of the revolutionary cause. These traits did not suddenly emerge in Stalin after 1924, but had been part of his character and existence from his earliest years as a Bolshevik.

Key

SSR (Soviet Socialist Republic)

1 Russian Soviet Federative Socialist Republic
2 Estonian SSR
3 Latvian SSR
4 Lithuanian SSR
5 Belorussian SSR
6 Ukrainian SSR
7 Moldavian SSR
8 Georgian SSR
9 Armenian SSR
10 Azerbaijan SSR
11 Kazakh SSR
12 Turkmen SSR
13 Uzbek SSR
14 Tajik SSR
15 Kirghiz SSR

Fig. 1 *The USSR under Stalin*

Although the Bolsheviks – or 'Reds' – had won the Civil War by 1921, Russia was in a sorry state. Most importantly, the economy was in ruins, the result of the devastation of war, mismanagement and lack of willing cooperation by peasants and workers. Industrial and agricultural production was well below pre-First World War levels. There was a major famine in 1921, resulting in millions of deaths. The Bolsheviks, now well established as the Communist Party, faced major revolts from peasants disillusioned with the requisitioning of their produce, and from Russians who wanted a genuine 'socialist democracy' rather than the centralised dictatorship of the Communist Party. Dissatisfaction was brought to a head in the 1921 revolt at the naval base of Kronstadt, led by former supporters of the Bolsheviks. Lenin also faced a hostile outside world that had failed to destroy the Bolsheviks during the Civil War. The world settled for a sullen blockade of the new Soviet State, but might pounce to take advantage of any weakness.

Lenin responded in two ways:

■ In March 1921 he announced the **New Economic Policy (NEP)**. This allowed small privately owned businesses to start up again, although not large-scale industries which remained under State control. Requisitioning of produce from the peasantry ceased. Instead, peasants were to pay tax, first in kind, and then in money. After paying tax, the peasants were free to dispose of extra produce as they wished, including the selling of produce in town markets.

■ Simultaneously, Lenin tightened control over the Communist Party. Although leading Communists were still free to argue about policy, rank and file members were expected to fall into line with the leadership's decisions. There were to be no groups, or 'factions' within the party, arguing for a particular line. The population as a whole had very little opportunity for free discussion, since the media was controlled by the State.

As far as the leadership was concerned, this combination of economic freedom and political authoritarianism worked. In the years of peace immediately following the Civil War, the economy picked up, particularly in the agricultural sector. Relations were gradually established with the outside world, including trade treaties and a secret treaty with Germany (The Treaty of Rapallo in 1922) allowing for military collaboration between Russia and Germany. At the same time, there was a new drive against internal opposition to the Bolsheviks. Remnants of other left-wing parties such as the Mensheviks and SRs were imprisoned or executed. Although many Communists were unhappy with the NEP, which they saw as an unwelcome compromise with free-market Capitalism, Lenin's leadership was unchallenged.

Lenin's apparent triumphs did not last long. He was never in the best of health after the 1917 Revolution. He was wounded in an assassination attempt and suffered a series of strokes that left him, after March 1923, virtually without the power of speech. In the last two years of his life, Lenin was pre-occupied with how the new Soviet State would be led after his death. He was worried about the excessive authoritarianism and bureaucracy within the party, both of which he had helped to create, but which he now saw as obstacles on the path to Socialism. Lenin doubted whether any of his comrades was fit to succeed himself as leader. His last will and testament criticised all his colleagues. He was particularly damning about Stalin, who had insulted Lenin's wife and was heavy handed and dictatorial in his behaviour. Stalin also controlled access to Lenin and controlled the party machine. Lenin probably assumed that Trotsky or some sort of collective leadership would succeed him, but he had not left a clear directive at the time of his death in January 1924. The way was open for Stalin and others to press their claims for leadership, or at least to decide how the still relatively new Soviet State should further develop.

Timeline

The colours represent different types of event as follows: Political and economic, Social and cultural

1924	1924	1924	1924	1924	1924	1924	1924
Death of Lenin. Stalin, Zinoviev and Kamenev block Trotsky from gaining a majority in the Politburo	Stalin publishes his *Foundations of Leninism*	Trotsky is isolated at the 13th Party Congress	The Central Committee agree not to publish Lenin's testament, thereby saving Stalin from disgrace or demotion	Petrograd is renamed Leningrad in honour of Lenin	Stalin publishes *Trotskyism or Leninism?*	The Comintern decide that all communist parties should follow the Russian model	New currency introduced

1926	1926	1926	1926	1927	1927	1927	1927
Zinoviev is expelled from the Politburo	Dzerzhinsky, Head of the GPU, dies	At the 15th Party Conference, Stalin attacks the United Opposition	Zinoviev and Kamenev are further demoted	Trotsky and Kamenev admit their guilt and are expelled from the Politburo. Kalinin, Molotov and Voroshilov join the Politburo	Trotsky and Zinoviev are expelled from the Central Committee and the party	Collectivisation is agreed at the 15th Party Conference	Stalin's marriage and family code is issued

1929	1929	1929	1929	1930	1930	1930	1930
The First Five Year Plan is presented at the 16th Party Conference	Bukharin is sacked from the Politburo	Stalin announces mass collectivisation and the 'liquidation of the kulaks'	Bukharin and his allies publically confess their 'errors'	The campaign against the kulaks is stepped up, until Stalin's 'Dizzy with Success' article calls for moderation in the process of collectivisation	The 16th Party Congress calls for the Five Year Plan to be completed in four years	It is announced that unemployment in the USSR has been eliminated	A trial is held of foreign engineers accused of sabotage

1925	1925	1925	1925	1925	1925	1926	1926
Trotsky is dismissed as Commissar for War	At the 14th Party Congress, Stalin argues for Socialism in One Country, whilst Bukharin declares that the peasants 'should enrich themselves'	Stalin's old comrade Voroshilov becomes Commissar for War	The official title of Communist Party of the Soviet Union (CPSU) is adopted	Zinoviev and Kamenev fail at the 14th Party Congress to overturn Stalin's industrialisation plans	The Central Committee pass a resolution for the control of literature. Eisentein's masterpiece *Battleship Potemkin* is released	Kirov replaces the sacked Zinoviev as Party Secretary in Leningrad	Stalin publishes *Questions of Leninism*. It becomes required reading in the party

1928	1928	1928	1928	1928	1928	1929	1929
Stalin introduces the Urals-Siberian method of grain requistioning	Trotsky is exiled to Alma Ata in Central Asia	Zinoviev and Kamenev denounce Trotsky	Collectivisation begins	The Shakhty show trials begin	Gorky returns to the USSR	Trotsky is exiled from the USSR, travelling to Turkey	Stalin attacks Bukharin and his supporters as counter-revolutionaries

1931	1932	1932	1932	1932	1932	1932	1932
Ex-Mensheviks and ex-SRs working in Gosplan are imprisoned	Famine strikes the USSR	Zinoviev and Kamenev are exiled to Siberia	The Ukrainian famine is at its peak	Stalin's wife commits suicide	Internal passports are introduced, except for peasants	Socialist Realism is proclaimed as the official art form	The Union of Soviet Writers is set up

1933	1933	1933	1933	1933	1934	1934	1934
Zinoviev and Kamenev are allowed back to Moscow	A mass purge of the party begins – one third is expelled	British engineers are put on trial	The White Sea Canal is opened	The Second Five Year Plan begins	Soviet successes are celebrated at the 17th Party Congress, the 'Congress of Victors'	The death penalty is made compulsory for treason, and families are made collectively responsible for their members	The GPU is reorganised as the NKVD

1935	1935	1936	1936	1936	1936	1936	1936
Almost 10 per cent of party members are expelled	The composer Sergei Prokofiev returns to the USSR	The Stalin Constitution is adopted	A show trial is held of Kamenev and Zinoviev and they are shot	Yezhov replaces the purged Yagoda as Head of the NKVD	It is announced that the USSR has attained Socialism	Tomsky commits suicide	Gorky dies

1939	1939	1940	1940	1941
Stalin declares the terror over at the 18th Party Congress	The USSR occupies eastern Poland and attacks Finland	The soviets execute thousands of Polish officers at Katyn	Trotsky is assassinated in Mexico	Germany attacks the USSR

1934	1934	1934	1934	1935	1935	1935	1935
Peasants are allowed private plots	Kirov is murdered in Leningrad and is replaced as Party Secretary by Zhdanov. A new terror begins	The first Congress of Soviet Writers is held	Sholokhov's *And Quiet Flows the Don* is published	Zinoviev and Kamenev are arrested	The Moscow Metro is opened	A popular front against Fascism is announced	The Stakhanovite programme begins

1937	1937	1937	1937	1938	1938	1938	1938
A show trial is held of Radek and several others	Ordzhonikidze commits suicide	A purge of the Red Army begins, and political commissars are attached to the army	Tukhachevsky and other leading officers are executed	Bukharin, Yagoda, Rykov and others are tried and shot	Beria takes over from Yezhov as Head of the NKVD	The Third Five Year Plan begins	Russian becomes a compulsory subject in all Soviet schools

1 Stalin's personal rule

Fig. 1 *Soviet propaganda poster showing Stalin with books*

In this chapter you will learn about:

- how Stalin rose to power, and the personal qualities that enabled him to do so

- the principal rivals whom Stalin had to overcome to achieve power following the death of Lenin

- how Stalin defeated opposition from the right and the left of the Communist Party

- the events that led up to the 'second revolution' of 1928.

Before they closed him in the tomb
Lost to the light of day,
Five days and nights stretched in the Hall
Of Columns still he lay.

The people filed in an endless train
With flags borne low at rest
To see his sallowing profile again
And the medal red on his chest.

And over the earth that he'd forsaken
So fierce a frost held sway
It seemed that he had surely taken
Part of our warmth away.

Five nights in Moscow no one slept
Because to sleep he had gone.
Close watch the sentinel moon kept,
Solemn and wan.

1   *A Soviet poem 'Five days and nights' by Vera Inber written in 1924 after the death of Lenin*

Stalin's rise to power between the death of Lenin and the beginning of the second revolution of 1928–9

The sources of Stalin's strengths

Stalin's rise to power did not begin with Lenin's death. His positions within the party had already given Stalin considerable influence. Of most significance was Stalin's position as General Secretary of the Party, which he had been given in 1922. It is doubtful whether the potential for influence given by this position was recognised at the time of Stalin's appointment. However, the party already had a much more important role than the State organisations that, in theory, managed the country. Stalin also had another major strength at this time. He was very close to Lenin during his final months, and virtually controlled access to the sick leader. He even had Lenin's office bugged in order to gain information – possibly an early sign of the paranoia so evident in the 1930s. Stalin compiled reports on other prominent Communists, including those who were to be his main rivals for power and influence. The massive increase in party membership begun in 1923 – the so-called 'Lenin Enrolment' – was managed by Stalin. The new party recruits owed loyalty to Stalin. Even so, Stalin was shrewd enough to keep out of major controversy. Even after Lenin's death, Stalin built up the cult of Lenin before promoting himself as Lenin's successor.

The struggle for power after Lenin's death was partly about policy, and partly about personalities. Stalin won the personal and policy battle. The policies he introduced or which became associated with his name were more in keeping with Soviet needs at the time than those of his rivals. As for personalities, Stalin was more than a match for other leading Communists – notably Zinoviev, Kamenev, Trotsky and Bukharin – although they did not realise this fact until it was too late. Stalin's supposedly more 'intellectual' rivals found it difficult to understand why they were defeated by Stalin, partly because they were vain and patronising towards him and underestimated both his ruthlessness and his abilities. They doubted his intellectual ability and the coarseness that came partly from his Georgian background. Comments from those like Trotsky who referred to Stalin as a 'grey blur', 'comrade card-index' or the 'arch-mediocrity' simply betrayed their own short-sightedness. Yet these interpretations of Stalin were to influence generations of historians. They tended to focus extensively on Stalin's ruthlessness, seen for example in his early revolutionary days when he organised violent bank raids to get money for the party. This ruthlessness was undoubtedly a key feature of Stalin's personality, but it has sometimes overshadowed his other qualities.

Fig. 2 *Joseph Stalin and Vladimir Lenin, 1919*

■ Cross-reference

The importance of the Communist Party and some of its major organisations like the Orgburo, Secretariat and Politburo, are explained on pages 136–7.

■ Key terms

Politburo: a small group of leading party members who, until Stalin became the acknowledged leader in 1929, met regularly to decide party and government policy.

Secretariat and **Orgburo:** these were two high-ranking party organisations responsible for supervising and carrying out decisions made by the party leadership.

Leningrad: Russia's second city, and its capital for over 200 years until 1918. Previously known as the northerly city of St Petersburg. During the First World War it was renamed Petrograd, to make it sound more Russian (meaning 'Peter's city', since it was built by Tsar Peter the Great). It was renamed Leningrad ('Lenin's city') after Lenin's death. After the break up of the USSR, it was renamed St Petersburg, thus coming full circle. Often known as the 'Venice of the North' for its beauty and many waterways.

Fig. 3 *Grigori Zinoviev, 1917*

Stalin's rise to power was a combination of political and personal ability, ambition, luck, and the mistakes or miscalculations of others.

Political and personal ability

By 1924, Stalin was already in a powerful position in the party. He was General Secretary, and also a member of the Orgburo, Secretariat and Politburo. The Politburo was the small decision-making body of the party, and the Orgburo and Secretariat carried out the decisions. Stalin was the only man to occupy all these positions simultaneously. Stalin made effective use of these opportunities:

■ As **General Secretary**, Stalin ran the party machine. As such, he occupied probably the most powerful single position in the USSR and could decide promotions to party positions.

■ As a member of the **Politburo**, Stalin was one of the small group of leading Communists who met regularly to make policy. They were effectively the decision makers for the USSR.

■ As a member of the **Secretariat** and the **Orgburo**, Stalin was also responsible for carrying out policy decisions and monitoring party personnel.

■ Between 1917 and 1923, Stalin was also **Commissar for Nationalities**. In this role, he supervised officials in the non-Russian republics that had been part of the old Russian Empire and now made up the territory of the USSR.

■ As Head of the **Workers' and Peasants' Inspectorate**, Stalin supervised the work of all government departments.

Stalin's rivals also held important posts. For example, Zinoviev was head of the party organisation in **Leningrad**, Russia's second city after Moscow. Trotsky was Commissar for War until 1925. But nobody else had the links or influence within the party as a whole that Stalin had. Equally important, Stalin knew how to use these links and opportunities effectively.

■ Key profile

Grigori Zinoviev

Zinoviev (1883–1936) was with Lenin in exile until April 1917, and returned with Lenin on the train to the Finland station in Petrograd. He then joined Kamenev in opposing Lenin's call for an uprising. Between 1918 and 1926, Zinoviev was influential as the head of the Leningrad Party organisation. He was allied with Kamenev first against Trotsky, and then with Trotsky and Kamenev in the United Opposition against Stalin after Lenin's death. Zinoviev was tried and imprisoned in 1935, given another trial in 1936 and then executed with Kamenev. Zinoviev was regarded more as an agitator than his more thoughtful colleague Kamenev.

Advantages in the struggle for power

■ Regarded as intelligent, energetic and with a wide knowledge of European culture.

■ One of the party's best speakers.

■ An 'Old Bolshevik' and therefore commanded respect from colleagues.

■ Promoted to the highest ranks of the party by Lenin, and one of Lenin's close associates, regarded by him as his 'closest and most trusted assistant'.

- Had important and influential positions in the Comintern, the Politburo and the Leningrad Party.

Disadvantages in the struggle for power

- Gained a reputation for inconsistency, seen in his opposition to Lenin in 1917 and switching alliances between Stalin and Trotsky.
- Seen as an ambitious compromiser, without a clear philosophy, someone who was vain but lacking in political courage, and he buckled under political pressure, e.g. in renouncing Trotskyism after defeat by Stalin in 1927.
- Subject to considerable and unpredicatable mood swings.
- Seriously underestimated his opponents, especially Stalin, whom he looked down upon.

Stalin demonstrated considerable political skills. After Lenin's death, he cleverly presented himself as the upholder of the former leader's legacy. He was instrumental in creating the Lenin cult, which included having Lenin's body enbalmed for display in Moscow's Red Square – a gesture of which Lenin himself would almost certainly have disapproved. The Lenin cult inspired a kind of religious fervour. Because Lenin was regarded as the fount of wisdom and the ultimate authority on Marxism, when Stalin began to use Lenin's name to justify his own policies, it was that much more difficult for colleagues to argue with him. Stalin arranged Lenin's funeral, delivered the funeral speech, and stated his determination to continue translating Lenin's ideas into practice, with himself interpreting what these ideas were. By these methods, some of Lenin's immense authority, which had derived not from any official position but from his record of having led Russia through revolution and civil war and from his reputation as the torchbearer of Marxist ideology, rubbed off on Stalin.

A closer look

Marxist ideology

Karl Marx had developed the initial theory of **Communism** in the 19th century. He believed that **Capitalism**, the economic and political system of countries like Britain and France at that time, was based on a class structure that allowed the middle and upper classes to run things for their own benefit. They controlled capital, or the means of production, and exploited the labour of the **proletariat** or working class so that they themselves could make huge profits.

Marx believed that eventually the working class, as it grew in size, would rise up against its bosses and establish a worker's state in which all were equal and exploitation would cease.

In more backward countries like Russia, in which the working class was very small compared to the peasants, Marxist believers like Lenin and Stalin insisted that the workers were not strong enough to carry out a revolution by themselves. They needed to be organised and led by a party of full-time professional revolutionaries. This party would bring about a revolution, then industrialise Russia so that it would develop a large working class, and the party would then establish **Socialism** – a society in which the State ran things for the benefit of the ordinary people. Eventually this would develop into Communism, a situation in which each person would

Key terms

Communism: the political, economic and social system towards which the Communist Party was working. It was to be a classless society in which all people were equal and working together for the common good, based upon the Marxist principle of 'From each according to his ability, to each according to his needs.'

Capitalism: the economic system from which most great world powers derived their strength. It was based on private ownership of the means of resources such as land and industry, with profits being made by the owners or 'Capitalists'. These would often hire workers who were paid wages which might be unrelated to the profits made by the owners.

Proletariat: a communist term meaning the industrial working class.

Socialism: for Marxists, this was the stage of development between Capitalism and Communism. Socialism was when the power of the capitalist class had been broken, and the 'State' (or Communist Party) took power and managed society and the economy in the interests of ordinary workers and peasants, rather than for personal profit, until class differences had disappeared. Then the State, with all its bureaucracy, would 'wither away', and there would be a transition to a full-blown communist society in which there was no centralised power.

work for the benefit of all. Then the organisation of the State, with its government departments, police, etc, would simply lose its functions so that the State would 'wither away'.

However, Marxists in Russia and elsewhere spent much of their time arguing exactly how these developments would take place, when would be the right time for revolution, how the party would gain more support, and so on. Lenin, Stalin and others were professional revolutionaries who were always seeking ways to accelerate the process of change in their favour.

In the ideological battle over future Soviet policy in the mid-1920s, Stalin was careful to present himself as the man of the centre, almost a moderate. He seemed to be able to avoid many of the bickerings of those rivals who argued about the path to Socialism and changed alliances. When Stalin did commit himself to a policy, notably '**Socialism in One Country**', it was a policy that had general appeal, because it meant that Russians could concentrate on their own problems and not worry about trying to change the rest of the world. Stalin also prepared the ground well before arguing a case. Party **congresses** were packed with his supporters – party members who, in most cases, owed their positions to him and whose details were certainly in the files that Stalin's party organisation kept. Contrary to the impression sometimes given, Stalin was capable of speaking quite eloquently or wittily (despite his thick Georgian accent) and with apparent conviction at important party gatherings like the annual congresses. Many of those who underestimated Stalin came to regret it later.

Ambition

Stalin gave few indications until the late-1920s that he was aiming for power. He had risen to prominence under Lenin not because he was regarded as a potential leader, but because he was a good second-rank party man who could be counted on to 'get things done', even the most difficult tasks, whilst more intellectual members of the party debated policies and decisions. Later commentators, working backwards from the 1930s and trying to explain Stalin's rise to power, sometimes credited him with unbridled ambition or a lust for power. That may have been part of Stalin's personality *after* he was in power. However, it is difficult to believe that Stalin was originally driven by a desire for power alone. Years before the revolution he had joined the insignificant Bolshevik Party, and what is more he was a **Georgian** and an outsider. A position of prominence must have seemed very unlikely. There probably was a point – was it before Lenin's death, at the time of Lenin's death or later? – when Stalin 'decided' or realised that he was at least the equal of his more prominent rivals, and then he showed the drive and other qualities to get to the top. What is more difficult to determine is whether, at this stage in the mid-1920s, Stalin was more concerned with establishing his own power over the party for reasons of personal ambition, or whether he was genuinely seeking power because he believed that he was the best man to lead the USSR on the path to Socialism. You might decide for yourselves by attempting the exercise at the end of this section.

Luck

Like most successful politicians, Stalin enjoyed some luck, especially during the 1920s when he was one of several leading Communists

■ **Key terms**

Congress: the Communist Party held regular congresses. Party delegates came from all over the USSR to listen to reports from leading party figures on policies and progress.

Georgian: Georgia was one of the Southern republics of the USSR. As a Georgian, Stalin was not a native Russian speaker, and his early writings, including poetry, were in the Georgian language, very different from Russian. Georgians were known for being typically more extrovert than Russians, and much given to family blood feuds.

■ **Cross-reference**

For more on the party structure and activities, see pages 136–7.

Fig. 4 *Joseph Stalin*

manoeuvring for power. One of the most crucial instances was after Lenin's death, when his colleagues decided not to publish Lenin's testament. This contained a damning criticism of Stalin, including references to the rough way in which he treated comrades, and even Lenin's own wife. The testament included a call to remove him from his leading positions in the party. To have published the testament to a wider audience would probably have been the end of Stalin's career at the top. But Trotsky and his colleagues decided against publication, mainly because they believed that party unity would be badly damaged and that Lenin's insistence on party unity and his banning of 'factions' (meaning groups within the party following a particular line) would be compromised if the testament became common knowledge. Stalin was aware that he had had a lucky escape, and went on to capitalise on his good fortune. Once in power, Stalin considerably reduced the likelihood of any such opportunities to unseat him from occurring again. On the contrary, he himself ruthlessly exploited any weaknesses shown by past or potential rivals. For example, the opposition of Zinoviev and Kamenev in 1917 to Lenin's decision to launch the October Revolution was used by Stalin as one of the ways of discrediting them during the struggle for power.

Key profile

Lev Kamenev

Kamenev (1883–1936) was one of the 'Old Bolsheviks', sent into exile in Siberia to the same setttlement where Stalin was exiled. Kamenev returned to Petrograd in 1917, where he allied with Zinoviev in opposing Lenin's idea of an armed uprising against the Provisional government, on the grounds that the Bolsheviks did not yet have enough popular support. After Lenin became ill in 1922, Kamenev joined Zinoviev and Stalin in opposing Trotsky. Kamenev had a power base in Moscow, where he ran the local party machine, but by 1927 he had lost his Moscow base and Stalin ended his political career. Kamenev renounced the Trotskyists and supported Stalin at the 1934 17th Party Congress. This did not save Kamenev: he was arrested after the Kirov assassination, given a show trial and executed in 1936.

Fig. 5 *Kamenev, who was accused of the assassination of Stalin's lieutenant Kirov*

Advantages in the struggle for power

- An 'Old Bolshevik', who helped form party policy and was close to Lenin – Lenin entrusted many of his personal papers to him in 1922.
- Had influence in Moscow where he ran the local party.
- Regarded as thoughtful and intelligent, good at smoothing out difficulties amongst colleagues, although less popular than Zinoviev.

Disadvantages in the struggle for power

- Like Zinoviev, gained reputation for inconsistency and opportunism by opposing Lenin in 1917 and switching alliances between Stalin and Trotsky.
- Regarded by many as too soft, without the wish or ability to be a leader.
- Seriously underestimated opponents, especially Stalin.

Key term

Left and right: these terms were in common use in Russia in the 1920s, as in many countries. In the USSR, the terms were used to describe people who were all members of the Communist Party, but took a different stance on certain things. Generally, being on the left meant that you supported radical or ruthless solutions to problems such as how to get grain from the peasantry. Generally, if you were on the right, you wanted a more moderate approach. However, both left and right wanted the same thing in the end – a Socialist and then a Communist Russia, so arguments were about means rather than ends.

Fig. 6 *Trotsky (1879–1940), Russian theoretician and politician*

The mistakes or miscalculations of others

For all Stalin's talents and determination, combined with the luck outlined on pages 14–15, his rise to power was also considerably aided by the tactical mistakes and shortcomings of his colleagues – weaknesses that Stalin exploited to the full. The weaknesses were shown by colleagues on both the **left** and **right** of the party. At the time, Trotsky seemed the most likely rival for power, because he had been Lenin's right-hand man during the revolution and the aftermath of the Civil War, and in that period he sometimes seemed to have had an even larger profile than Lenin. However, he was no match for Stalin, and any ambitions that Trotsky had were crushed by the mid-1920s, although he never accepted the fact until much later, if at all.

Trotsky: the lost leader?

Trotsky (his real name was Lev Bronstein) was born into a prosperous Jewish family. Jews were traditionally persecuted in Russia and, like many educated Jews, Trotsky was attracted into revolutionary politics. He was soon arrested and exiled in the interior of Russia. He was initially attracted to Lenin, but in 1903 joined the Mensheviks. After years of revolutionary politics and exile, Trotsky arrived back in Petrograd in May 1917. He joined the Bolsheviks and played a crucial role in planning and carrying out the Bolshevik seizure of power in the October Revolution.

Activity

Group activity

1 Each group decide on four examples which illustrate how each of the following four factors helped in Stalin's rise to power. Rank each factor in order of importance and justify your choice.

■ Political and personal ability

■ Ambition

■ Luck

■ The mistakes or miscalculations of others

2 This could then form the basis of a class debate or an essay on how and why Stalin became leader of the USSR by 1929.

Activity

Talking point

1 In groups, take one of the contenders for power, and discuss their relative strengths and weaknesses.

2 Research Trotsky's career and debate this question: 'Why did Trotsky not become leader of the USSR?'

After the revolution, Trotsky was prominent in Lenin's new Russia. He was Commissar for War and served in the Politburo alongside Stalin. Trotsky played a crucial role in the Civil War, creating the Red Army and leading it to victory. In the process, he fell out with Stalin. Stalin objected to Trotsky's employment of ex-tsarist officers and disobeyed his orders. After initial doubts about exploiting the peasants, Trotsky supported the rigorous application of War Communism, and crushed the 1921 Kronstadt Rebellion. This was a revolt by sailors and others who had initially fought for the Bolsheviks but had become disillusioned with their dictatorship. Trotsky tried to persuade Lenin that the NEP was not sufficient to resurrect the Soviet economy, and that full-scale planning was necessary. During Lenin's illness in 1922, Trotsky faced an opposition alliance of Stalin, Zinoviev and Kamenev, all afraid of Trotsky's influence and ambition.

Fig. 7 *A Soviet anti-Trotsky cartoon, showing Trotsky as an agent of the Nazis and with his hands steeped in blood*

Fig. 8 *Propaganda poster by Alexei Kokorekin: 'Long live the Red Army, protector of the assets of the October Revolution', 1933*

In the power struggle that followed Lenin's death, Trotsky had advantages and disadvantages:

Advantages

- Trotsky was clever, a dynamic speechmaker, and had shown himself to be an energetic man of action between 1917 and 1921.
- He had been Lenin's right-hand man during the revolution and the Civil War.
- He demonstrated a combination of formidable leadership skills, ruthlessness and decision-making abilities during these key years – for example in carrying out the October Revolution and leading the **Red Army**.

Key term

Red Army: the name given to the army formed by Trotsky to fight the Bolsheviks' enemies during the Civil War. It remained the guardian of the USSR's external security thereafter, although it was often subjected to political interference by the Communist Party.

Fig. 9 *Leon Trotsky during a party meeting, 1923*

Disadvantages

- Trotsky was a late convert to Bolshevism (in 1917) – which made some 'Old Bolsheviks' suspect him.

- Several leading Bolsheviks disliked his perceived aloofness, arrogance and disdain for those less clever than himself.

- Trotsky made no attempt to build a base of support within the party – a crucial mistake when it came to the party in-fighting after Lenin's death. It meant, for example, that Trotsky had a difficult time in the 1920s when confronting party congresses packed with Stalin's supporters.

- There was a fear among many Bolsheviks that Trotsky might use his Red Army links to mount a military, Napoleonic-style coup after Lenin's death. This was ironic given that after the Civil War, Trotsky was not very popular with Red Army leaders who felt that Trotsky was neglecting their interests.

- Trotsky himself believed that, as a Jew, there would be prejudice against him as leader because of traditional **anti-Semitism** in Russia. Therefore he did not push himself forward – although several other leading Bolsheviks such as Kamenev and Zinoviev were also Jewish.

- Trotsky laid himself open to the charge of being an opportunist who lacked consistency. For example, he attacked the growth of party bureaucracy in early 1924, which could be interpreted as a criticism of Lenin, and he was opposed by the 'Triumvirate' of Stalin, Kamenev and Zinoviev. Yet, after Lenin's death, he sided with his former opponents, Zinoviev and Kamenev, against Stalin.

- Trotsky was unpredictable. For all his brilliance, he could at times be indecisive and on some occasions showed a failure of nerve. He sometimes fell ill at critical moments: although his illnesses were sometimes genuine, there is a suggestion that on other occasions they may have been psychosomatic.

Key term

Anti-Semitism: there was a tradition of anti-Semitism in Russia, long pre-dating the revolution. There were many Jews living in Russia, and they had often been made scapegoats to divert people's attention from problems. Some supporters of the tsarist regime had organised fatal attacks against Jews known as *pogroms* (a Russian word meaning 'racially-inspired attack'). Because of their treatment, a number of educated Jews had joined revolutionary groups such as the Bolsheviks.

■ Trotsky made crucial errors of judgement. He attacked the party bureaucracy in 1924 when he needed its support. He argued against publicising Lenin's testament and thereby reprieved Stalin. He attacked Lenin's NEP in his book *Lessons of October* in 1924.

■ Above all, Trotsky completely underestimated Stalin, whom he regarded as his inferior, and never really came to terms with this.

■ Cross-reference

Compare to Interpretations of Stalin's rise to power on pages 24–6.

A closer look

Interpretations of Trotsky

'Trotskyism' became a term of abuse in Stalin's USSR, and was a convenient label to stick on anyone whom Stalin's regime wanted to discredit. Yet, it was also a label that has persisted down to this day for a wide range of political activists who admired some of the original ideals of the Russian revolutionaries but were strongly opposed to totalitarian regimes such as that of Stalin, which they regarded as the complete opposite of what a free socialist society should be like. Because Trotsky never got to a position in which he could exercise real political power, we have no way of knowing how a Trotsky-led regime might have operated. It would be dangerous to assume that it would have been any less authoritarian than the regimes of Lenin or Stalin, but historians have still argued about Trotsky's legacy. Sources 2 and 3 provide two interpretations.

Before his death, he [Trotsky] had denied the dogma of party infallibility; the claim of the party to represent the revolution, the right of the party to the government of the Soviet Union... He speaks for the power of people against those who speak for the power of the state. He speaks against privilege to those who speak for the subservience of others. He speaks for the liberation of ideas... He speaks for the will to resist... Trotsky speaks still for humanity... Trotsky bears witness to the creative force of that essential revolutionary, the integral man.

2 *R. Segal, **The Tragedy of Leon Trotsky**, 1983*

Trotskyism is an expression of Lenin's belief that it was possible by means of unbridled violence 'to give history a shove' and to achieve fundamental social change in the shortest possible time... Trotsky was one of the most consistent advocates of the 'traditional' violent solution of world problems... He firmly believed, with Lenin, in the dictatorship of one party, and in its monopoly on power, ideas and all decision-making, the very factors leading to the emergence of totalitarianism... In his tireless and passionate struggle with Stalin, he facilitated Stalin's seizure of power in the Party... It was Trotsky's own doing that allowed Stalin to surround himself with a circle of schismatics, heretics and other 'internal enemies.' ...He helped Stalin to become a bloody dictator.

3 *D. Volkogonov, **Trotsky: The Eternal Revolutionary**, 1996*

■ Activity

Thinking point

Create three columns labelled 'True', 'Possibly true' and 'False'. Consider the following statements about Trotsky and place each statement in the appropriate column. You may be asked to justify any of these statements!

1 Trotsky was the most gifted of all the contenders for power in the USSR in the 1920s.

2 Trotsky was Lenin's designated heir to succeed him as leader.

3 Trotsky inspired more distrust in the party than any other leading Communist in the 1920s.

4 Trotsky's role in the USSR before 1924 was crucial to the Communists' survival.

5 Trotsky had ceased to be important in the USSR long before he went into permanent exile.

6 Trotsky was responsible for his failure to defeat Stalin.

7 Trotsky was more effective as a thinker than as a man of action.

8 Trotsky did not understand Russia's needs in the 1920s.

9 Trotsky was not a convinced Bolshevik.

10 Trotsky did not do enough to create support for his views in the USSR.

11 Trotsky was consistent in his policies throughout the 1920s.

12 Trotsky lacked ambition.

13 Trotsky's views were totally rejected by Stalin.

14 Trotsky was cleverer than Stalin.

15 Trotsky was more important in exile than when he was in the USSR.

■ Key profile

Nikolai Bukharin

Bukharin (1888–1938) was an intellectual and a thinker. Lenin regarded him as 'the most valuable theoretician in the party'. Although Bukharin jusified War Communism, he later supported the NEP. After Lenin's death he was the most influential member of the party alongside Stalin, supported Stalin's Socialism in One Country and opposed Trotsky. He helped Stalin defeat the Left or United Opposition. Bukharin now supported the 'soft' approach to Socialism: that is, supporting the peasants' attempts to prosper, and thereby pay for later industrial development. In 1928, Bukharin was easily outmanoeuvred by Stalin, who by then was set on collectivisation. Although Bukharin, along with Tomsky and Rykov, renounced his views, his influence declined. However, Stalin had not forgotten his opposition: in 1937 Bukharin was expelled from the Central Committee, then in 1938 was tried and executed for treason.

Advantages in the struggle for power

■ Popular within the party, close to Lenin, and for a long time friendly with Trotsky.

■ Intelligent and regarded as the best thinker in the party.

■ For many years, a very close associate of Stalin and respected by him.

Fig. 10 *Nikolai Bukharin, member of the Communist Party and the Politburo and editor of the newspaper* Pravda *for a time. In 1938, he was tried publicly for treason and was executed*

■ Activity

Thinking point

Decide whether Zinoviev, Kamenev or Bukharin had the best claim to be the next leader of the USSR after Lenin. Justify your reasons.

- Stalin relied extensively on Bukharin's knowledge of economics.

Disadvantages in the struggle for power

- Naive and lacked the qualities of intrigue, making him unsuited to party in-fighting.
- Made the mistake of appearing to be more popular in the party than Stalin.
- In trying to remain loyal to everyone and avoiding taking sides in the factional in-fighting, he lacked a power-base.
- Seriously underestimated Stalin.
- Made a tactical mistake in 1928 by trying to establish links with the defeated Kamenev and appearing inconsistent.

Activity

Challenge your thinking

After you have studied the events of the 1930s, consider the following question:

Do you think the USSR would have developed differently had another Communist, such as Trotsky or Bukharin, become leader instead of Stalin?

As we shall see, Stalin's qualities enabled him to rise to a position of unrivalled power by 1928. By this time he was not yet the all-powerful dictator. He still had to listen to colleagues and could not do exactly as he wished without explaining his policies and motives. He could drive opponents out of the government but not yet physically eliminate them. Nevertheless, the days of genuine discussion between party colleagues about policy direction were over, and Stalin was free to begin his 'second revolution', the economic and social transformation of the USSR.

Stalin's defeat of the Left and Right Opposition and establishment of personal rule between 1924 and 1929

The defeat of the left

By the late-1920s, Stalin was well on the way to achieving power.

The four years following Lenin's death in 1924 saw considerable manoeuvring and shifting alliances amongst leading Communists. Following Trotsky's attack on the party bureaucracy in 1924, Stalin allied himself with Zinoviev and Kamenev against Trotsky, still seen after Lenin's death as a potential threat to the new regime. Arguments over policy followed. Trotsky argued for **permanent revolution**, which meant a focus on encouraging and helping revolutions abroad, so that the USSR would not be an isolated revolutionary State, alone in a hostile world. In 1925, Stalin began to champion the policy of Socialism in One Country, which meant the USSR concentrating on developing its strength and following its own path to Socialism, making itself formidable enough to discourage attacks by hostile Capitalist States. Trotsky attacked Stalin's ideas and joined Kamenev and Zinoviev in the **United** or **Left Opposition**. This alliance argued for a more rapid transition from the NEP to a Socialist State, which meant a commitment to rapid industrialisation. It was now that Stalin's growing power in the party proved invaluable. In 1926, the Left Opposition failed to get its policies accepted at the 15th Party Conference. This signalled the start of the rapid decline of the Left Opposition, which could no longer voice its policies publically. The left's leaders were expelled from their official positions and from the Politburo. Although Zinoviev and Kamenev remained in the party, they were effectively silenced. Trotsky would not be silenced, so was sent into internal exile before being forced to leave the USSR for good in 1929.

Fig. 11 *Satirical cartoon on a Soviet session, showing Trotsky on the right, Kalinin in the gallery and Stalin beating up Kamenev*

A closer look

Trotsky in exile

In the years following his expulsion from the USSR, Trotsky settled in France, Norway and eventually Mexico. He continued to write, denouncing what he saw as Stalin's perversion of the original Bolshevik ideals, as well as writing a history of the revolution and his autobiography. However, he failed to build a serious opposition movement against Stalin. Instead, his *own* family and colleagues in the USSR were ruthlessly eliminated in the 1930s terror.

The Soviet authorities eventually sent a Spanish Communist, Ramon Mercader, to assassinate Trotsky in Mexico. Mercader gained entrance to Trotsky's house on a pretext and then smashed an ice-pick into Trotsky's skull. Trotsky died the following day. 300,000 people filed past his coffin as his body lay in state for five days. The Soviet newspaper *Pravda* simply noted that Trotsky had been killed by a 'disillusioned follower'. Mercader was sentenced to 20 years in prison, and was released in 1960. He was then made a hero of the Soviet Union, but finished his career as a radio repair man in Czechoslovakia.

After Trotsky's death, 'Trotskyism' became a catchword for many left-wing movements that supported the ideals of the Russian Revolution but were bitterly opposed to totalitarian regimes such as Stalin's, as it was based largely on force and propaganda. Yet, Trotsky himself had been more than willing to use force to promote a cause in which he fanatically believed, for example during the Civil War and the crushing of the Kronstadt Rebellion.

The defeat of the right

Stalin overcame the left by using his power-base in the party and with the support of the right, led by Bukharin, Rykov and Tomsky. Bukharin, the chief spokesman of this group, had changed his views since the years immediately after the revolution, when he had welcomed the prospect of a rapid approach to the promised land of Socialism and the classless society. Like all Communists, Bukharin believed in the necessity of creating an industrialised USSR – otherwise there would be no basis for a socialist society that would offer wealth and create a working class that would, in turn, create the conditions for a transition to Communism. However, Bukharin did not believe that the USSR could push through rapid industrialisation, particularly if this involved the use of force. The USSR was still a peasant-based society. The peasants must be encouraged to produce more, and pay more tax, and the revenue could then be used to speed up industrial development, but at a pace that ensured social harmony. Bukharin believed that a ruthless approach of the sort practised under War Communism 10 years before would simply alienate a crucial sector of the population and could lead to disaster.

Fig. 12 *Leon Trotsky among a group of Trotskyists (his last days in Moscow)*

Key profiles

Alexei Rykov

Rykov (1881–1938) was a more moderate Bolshevik who had supported the idea of a coalition with other socialists in 1917. He was in the Politburo, and succeeded Lenin as Head of Government (The Council of People's Commissars) between 1924 and 1930. A member of Bukharin's right grouping, Rykov was given a show trial and executed in 1938.

Mikhail Tomsky

Tomsky (1880–1936) was a working-class Bolshevik who was put in charge of trade unions in 1919. Popular in the party, he was one of the pall bearers at Lenin's funeral. Hostile to the left, he found himself allied with Bukharin and was expelled from the Politburo in 1929. In 1936, he committed suicide when he discovered that the authorities were making enquiries about him.

Fig. 13 *Alexei Rykov*

Activity

Thinking point

Decide whether the main threat to Stalin's rise came from the left or the right. Find at least five points to justify your decision.

Unfortunately for those like Bukharin, the defeat of the left removed any dependence Stalin might have had on the right. In 1928, with Trotsky and the left effectively out of the picture, Stalin committed himself to rapid industrialisation, the policy previously of the left. When the right opposed Stalin's decision, Stalin simply had its leaders removed from the Politburo. Stalin was now effectively the leader of the USSR.

Summary of why Stalin came to power

The 1920s are sometimes presented as a struggle for power amongst competing personalities. There were personal rivalries, and not just that of Stalin against Trotsky. However, for the great majority of Communists, the struggle was not about personality but about policy, the direction in which the USSR should go. There had to be this debate, because no Communist could accept that the NEP represented the ideal society. It was a temporary measure that had helped to stabilise the USSR after a difficult time in its infancy. There must be substantial changes if the country were to progress through industrialisation and the creation of a strong State with a large working class. This would form the basis of a socialist society that, in turn, would create the conditions for an eventual classless, communist society. Therefore arguments about whether the USSR should concentrate on developing Socialism at home as a priority, or focus on spreading revolution abroad, or whether peasants should provide the money and labour for industrialisation, were very real. They were not just convenient slogans spouted by rivals for power. Nevertheless, it sometimes appeared that way because influential figures within the party did change policies. For example, Bukharin moved from being a hardline supporter of War Communism to a belief in encouraging the peasants to 'get rich'. Most notably, Stalin sometimes took over other people's ideas, for example the left's approach of drastic action in support of industrialisation and against the peasantry. Does that mean that the actual arguments were irrelevant to him?

One of the reasons why there was strong rivalry between leading Communists was simply that they wanted to keep out of power those people who put forward policy views with which they themselves profoundly disagreed. It would be too simplistic to say that Stalin was simply out for power for power's sake, just because he sometimes changed his views. The same could be said of almost all Communists. This is hardly surprising, given that the USSR was a great experiment: there was no blueprint for success and there was no example of another country that had gone through a similar political and economic revolution and from which the USSR could learn. It is also important to note that Stalin did not just have the advantages of control of the party and the skill to take advantage of his rivals' weaknesses and then outmanoeuvre them. Stalin also had popular support. He was putting forward policies with which most party members agreed. This was true even of the hardline policy towards the peasantry adopted in the late-1920s.

Interpretations of Stalin's rise to power

Historians writing about Stalin outside of Russia have tended to fall into one of two camps. Some focus on the role of individuals like Stalin himself or his rivals like Trotsky, seeing their decisions and interaction as the most important factors in major developments such as industrialisation and collectivisation.

Others prefer to put less emphasis on the role of individuals and instead analyse developments in the Communist Party. This interpretation is sometimes called a structuralist approach, because it focuses on the structure of the party. One historian who focused extensively on the nature of the Communist Party was Edward Carr, who played down the role of personal ambition. Such historians take the view that the party developed in a particular direction immediately after the revolution, and that many of its key characteristics, such as intolerance of opposition, and the fact that decisions were made by the leadership and then passed down, were firmly in place under Lenin. Many Western historians like Robert Service have analysed the continuities in the Soviet regime between Lenin and Stalin. Stalin took the policies and the party in a more 'extreme' direction, but he was building on something already in place, not starting anew. A variant on this theme also plays down the role of personalities because some historians prefer to focus on social, economic and cultural trends, which to some extent developed independently of personalities, even though individuals like Stalin clearly did initiate change. Some historians in this mould take the Trotskyist line that Stalin was a product of the circumstances of the time, and in creating a **bureaucratic State** he was responding to changes already taking place in the economy and society.

Key term

Bureaucratic State: 'bureaucratism' was a charge often levelled against the USSR by its opponents. It meant a society that was so dominated by the governing bureaucracy (in effect the party), that maintaining the bureaucracy almost became an end in itself, rather than using it to further the interests of ordinary people.

Soviet historians before 1985 were influenced heavily by the political climate under which they wrote. Therefore, whilst alive, Stalin was projected as a genius who was leading the country securely on the path to Communism, building on the great achievements already begun by Lenin. Under Khrushchev and later Soviet leaders, this approach was modified: whilst accepting that the general line of Soviet policy was correct, and was taking the USSR on the road to a better society, there was some criticism of Stalin as having overreached himself, for example in the way he dealt with rivals. Since the collapse of the USSR in 1991, Russian historians have been much stronger in their criticisms of Stalin. Whilst accepting to some extent that Stalin reflected unfortunate trends already evident in the party, such as excessive bureaucracy that ignored the wellbeing of individuals, there was also strong criticism of Stalin's ruthlessness, although most criticism was reserved for his excesses as dictator in the 1930s, once he was securely in power. Dmitri Volkogonov, a former Red Army officer as well as a historian, was very critical of Stalin, although he also conceded like many British historians that there was continuity with the Russia of Lenin.

Activity

Thinking point

Consider the different interpretations of Stalin outlined on page 24 and opposite. Find two pieces of evidence to support each interpretation, and two pieces of evidence to argue against that interpretation. Which interpretation seems to you to be the most convincing?

The truth is that Stalin was a complex character. It may be that he did genuinely accept the NEP as a 'necessary evil' in the early 1920s, and then changed his view when he realised that it was not working (Chapter 2, pages 36–8). This could be regarded as sensible development of policy rather than opportunism or lack of principle, charges that have sometimes been levelled against Stalin.

A closer look

Stalin's take over of Moscow

Whilst studying the rivalries of leading Communists may give a reasonably clear overall picture of Stalin's rise to power, there has been less focus on what happened in particular places or regions. Analysing what happened in the Soviet capital, Moscow, may give us some indication of how Stalin manoeuvred himself into power.

Until October 1928, the Moscow Party organisation was controlled by the right, under the local party secretary N. A. Uglanov. His opponents then defeated him through a mixture of blackmail and threats, whilst his position was also weakened by an economic recession in the late-1920s that led to a 25 per cent unemployment rate amongst adult males. Trotsky's supporters had already been removed from Moscow. The new first party secretary in Moscow from 1929 was Karl Bauman, who was every bit as ruthless as Stalin himself turned out to be. Bauman was the first to coin the phrase 'liquidation of the kulaks as a class'. Bauman's officials were anxious to prove their loyalty and show that they had no sympathies with the right. Consequently, they carried out collectivisation of agriculture in their region so ruthlessly that the Central Committee stepped in and sacked Bauman and over 100 of his officials. Bauman was, in turn, succeeded by Lazar Kaganovich, a loyal Stalinist. To ensure that Stalin's policies were followed, the Moscow Party was disciplined, with a halt to recruitment to the party there, and with police officials attending party meetings. Many of the new breed of Communists were working in Stalin's interests, but were energetic and confident enough to sometimes act without his direct orders.

Summary questions

1. Explain why there was no clear successor to Lenin in 1924.
2. Explain why Trotsky did not become leader of the USSR.
3. Explain why Stalin came to power by 1929.

2   The USSR on the eve of the Stalin revolution

In this chapter you will learn about:

- how the economy was organised and performed in NEP Russia

- the political and economic reasons why Stalin decided to carry out an economic revolution in the USSR.

Activity

As a class, can you explain these comments by peasants (Sources 1 and 2)?

When we arrive at socialism, will there be one cow, two cows, several cows, or no cows at all?

| **1** | *A question asked by a peasant at a district Congress meeting in 1925* |

We are fed up with your tales. The only thing you've learned in seven years is blab. You are not improving agriculture but ruining it. You, Red executioners, you'd better know that the steam engine of peasant patience is going to explode some day. You'd better know that the peasants curse you usurpers in their morning prayer. You are stealing the last cow, the last belongings. What do you say to a peasant invalid who had lost a leg defending your revolution? You can't pay a rouble to him, but to a Tsarist general you pay 300. Where is truth? Where is justice? Why did you fool us with words such as freedom, land, peace, equality? Now we understand that the government of Kerensky was better to us.

| **2** | *A peasant's complaint at a Congress election meeting in 1925* |

The state of the NEP economy in 1928

Arguments for the NEP

Fig. 1 *Propaganda poster by Mikhail Deregus: 'Let us prepare the harvest', 1930*

The NEP, or the New Economic Policy, was not regarded by any Communist as a permanent state of affairs. It had been introduced in 1921 essentially as an emergency measure to rescue the economy and possibly the communist regime itself from a condition of economic collapse and growing unpopularity arising out of the Civil War years. Lenin admitted this, although he later tried to give the NEP another justification by arguing that it was a logical 'halfway house' between the Capitalism that the revolution had set out to destroy and the future era of Socialism. This era would take a long time to establish in a Russia seriously lacking in large-scale, modern industrial development. Lenin's stance had some logic since the NEP was a mixture of the private economy, with its toleration of peasant enterprise and small-scale private ownership in industry, and 'public' or rather State-owned industry in major sectors like mining and the railways. The NEP allowed individuals the opportunity to make money and do well for themselves by showing initiative, whilst in theory it also protected the interests of the population as a whole since the key industries and means of production and distribution were in State hands. Therefore the State was supposed to be looking after the interests of the ordinary man and woman, although not all Communists, nor the rest of the population, were convinced that this was the case.

Arguments against the NEP

As already indicated, the arguments for the NEP did not carry much weight with many Communists. These doubters took

Cross-reference

For more on the origins of the NEP, see pages 4–5.

See pages 13 and 14 for explanations of Capitalism and Socialism as defined by Marxists.

Key term

Bourgeoisie: means the middle class. 'Bourgeois' was often used by Communists almost as a term of abuse, to attack the class of people such as private traders, bankers, industrialists, and others considered to be exploiting 'ordinary' people in order to make a profit from them.

Activity

Make a list of the NEP's strengths and weaknesses as they might have appeared to the following individuals in the mid-1920s USSR:

- a peasant
- an industrial worker
- a housewife
- a priest
- a Communist Party member.

Marxist ideology seriously. In their eyes, the economic base of the NEP was deeply flawed, since private enterprise meant that some people were making a profit out of others' labour or out of pure speculation. This went totally against the principle of public good. However, it was even worse than that. Economic divisions meant that class differences were perpetuated or even increased: the 'new **bourgeoisie**' appeared, making money and recalling memories of pre-revolutionary Russia. These people were parasites, not wealth creators. They were enemies of Socialism, and the USSR could not move forward confidently into a socialist future if not everyone had the same vision of society. Class differences could lead to political divisions and the end of the great communist experiment. It was hardly surprising therefore that there were so many political arguments about the correct path ahead. These arguments were also bound up with, and sometimes distorted by, political ambition. Although there were significant differences of opinion as to how Socialism should be brought about, all party members agreed that the NEP experiment could not last forever.

How the Soviet economy developed between 1924 and 1928

Agriculture

Fig. 2 *Famine in Stavropol, on the banks of the Volga. Russian peasants showing their distress to foreign journalists*

By the early 1920s, Soviet agriculture had suffered severely from the devastation of War Communism and the Great Famine of 1921–2. Added to this, was the disruption and terror caused by the activities of partisans living in the forests, deportations, executions and the burning of villages by the authorities seeking out 'counter-revolutionaries'. The situation was not stabilised until 1923. Thereafter, there had been a swift recovery and, by 1926, production had mostly recovered to pre-First World War levels. Many peasant households benefited from the freedom to sell produce on the open market after paying tax. However, this positive picture concealed several problems and raised concerns:

- Recovery was uneven. Production in the central and southern regions recovered much more slowly than in the eastern and northern regions. The recovery in production of certain crops such as sugar beet, fruit and vegetables was much more dramatic than the recovery of grain production.

- Because richer peasants were taxed more heavily than poorer peasants, and the taxes were based on the size of herds, fields and estimated harvests, many peasants tried to hide as many of their possessions as they could, such as stocks of grain. The authorities raised only about four fifths of their target figures and sometimes resorted to direct requisitioning as in the days of War Communism. The peasantry remained unhappy. The security police (GPU) frequently reported complaints by peasants that, although the NEP was better than War Communism, they were taxed more than they had been under the Tsar. Peasants also complained that, despite the promise of free trade, local authorities often tried to control the prices that peasants charged when they went into the nearest town to sell their produce at private markets.

- Farmers kept more of the produce for themselves. Only about half the amount of grain that had been sold outside the villages in 1913 was sold in this way in 1926. Surplus food meant lower food prices, and peasants were reluctant to sell food in order to buy more expensive and scarcer industrial goods. They were more likely to reduce the amount of land they cultivated. Meanwhile, peasants sold most of their meat and dairy produce privately, and this could not be controlled by the government, which in contrast had much more control over grain production. This was a major cause of the 1927–8 grain crisis, the so-called **procurement** crisis, which pushed the regime into requisitioning (the 'Urals-Siberian method', named after the area of Russia in which it began) and then into collectivisation. Collectivisation was the merging of smaller farms into much larger units, as is explained on pages 69–70. There is also some evidence that Stalin exaggerated the crisis in order to provide an excuse for tough action against the peasantry.

- Exports fell. Grain exports were only a quarter of the 1913 level. This meant less revenue coming into the USSR.

- The great majority of peasant households (which totalled about 23 million in 1926) still farmed in a relatively primitive way: they used a strip system and three-field rotation system of farming, similar to that practised in England in the Middle Ages, except that in Russia the village commune or *mir* decided which households got what land and when, what crops should be grown and when they should be harvested. Machinery was scarce, and three-quarters of arable land was sown by hand and then harvested by sickles and scythes. The only freedom peasants had was to decide what to buy and sell, and if they were wealthy enough, what labour to employ. It was a system of small-scale individual peasant farming, which could not support the ambitious plans for industrialisation.

- Frequent peasant complaints, collected and monitored by party organs like the security police, show continuing hostility by the peasantry. Peasants complained of discrimination not just in taxation but in areas such as education and medical care. One peasant reported at his village meeting:

> In the old times there were two classes in Russia, the bourgeoisie and the second class, workers and peasants. And now we also have two classes, the Communists and the peasants. Access to everything is open to the first, but nothing is open to us.

> **Key term**
>
> **Procurement:** so-called because the State 'procured' or acquired foodstuffs from the peasantry – either peacefully or through compulsion.

The leading Communist Molotov was shown a letter from a peasant in Kostroma province:

> Why is it that the party is preaching to the peasants about collective labour, about the future of Communism and Socialism, but the party itself, both the central and the local one, does not practise this and does not even strive to? Party officials live by themselves separately in private apartments… They receive all kinds of salaries and they have servants… They enjoy all the benefits of life just as the old civil servants.

■ Between 1924 and 1927, peasant unions were set up all over Russia to try to defend peasant interests. They were all destroyed by the authorities. However, it was worrying for the authorities that in some areas local Communists, who had ties with the local community, expressed sympathy or even support for these unions, since they themselves seem to have felt oppressed by policies coming from Moscow.

■ In the 1925 local congress elections in the countryside, the Communists made great efforts but did very badly. Instead of party members, amongst those elected were kulaks, teachers and a whole range of candidates. Once elected, they often refused to accept party directives but sometimes engaged instead in 'counter-revolutionary' activities such as repairing desecrated churches.

■ The fact that farming was individual, with millions of peasants involved, made it difficult for the largely urban-based Communist Party to control what went on in the countryside. The party was very thinly spread in the countryside. In Orel, there were only 1,595 party members, two-thirds of them illiterate, out of a population of hundreds of thousands; similarly in Kursk there were 3,320 members, mostly 'politically illiterate'. The rural police were difficult to recruit, were thinly spread, poorly equipped and incapable of effective law enforcement. The authorities distinguished between 'poor peasants', meaning those too poor to support a family from their own land, and kulaks, who were regarded as exploiters of the poor. However, the regime was not very successful in driving a wedge between the two classes and persuading the poorer peasants that the regime was their protector. Peasants were far more outspoken than city dwellers in their criticisms of the communist regime, and clearly often saw through communist propaganda to the realities of their situation.

Fig. 3 *Russian peasants*

Peasant complaints

The GPU collected lists of the most common complaints and questions made by peasants at local meetings, including Soviets, in NEP Russia. The following are just a selection:

■ Why is it that only the intelligentsia get into the institutions of higher learning, and it is hard for peasants to be accepted?

■ Why is it that only Jews are sent to the hospitals but for peasants it is virtually impossible?

■ Why are the majority of officials Communist Party members?

- How much is paid to the people's commissars [a communist term meaning ministers or high-ranking officials]?
- Why are Communists armed?
- Why was the tax last year 550 roubles and this year 800?
- What is the amount of grain exported abroad?
- Where is Trotsky? Is he a member of the CP [Communist Party]?
- Why is it not allowed to hang religious icons in schools?
- Where did the valuables removed from the Church go?
- Why are peasants not covered by social insurance?
- Why is it that in other countries there are peasant unions and here we can't have them?
- Why is there no freedom of speech?
- What did the revolution give to peasants?
- Is it possible to equalise human talents and bring everyone to the same level?
- Why is tax now three times as high as under the Tsar?
- What was the goal of the NEP and what has been achieved?
- On whose orders are the priests persecuted?
- Why is a peasant who owns two cows considered a kulak [the Russian term for a rich peasant]?
- How long are you going to torture the peasantry?
- What happened to your promises?
- How long are you going to hang around our necks as parasites?
- When will the Soviet power cease ruining peasant agriculture?
- What do we need the world revolution for? And why should we care about it?

Quoted in Brovkin, V. *Russia After Lenin*, 1998

Activity

Thinking point

Choose six complaints or questions from the above list. Decide what they tell you about popular attitudes towards both life in Russia at the time and the communist regime.

The party became alarmed. In several areas of the USSR its policies were being defied, and this had been confirmed by the 1925 elections to rural Soviets. The party leadership blamed the influence of 'kulaks', and made a decision in 1926, long before collectivisation, to destroy the kulaks as a class. The first step was to tax them much more heavily, then they lost their civil rights, and then in 1928 many were given hard labour, had their property confiscated and their children deprived of schooling. This was two years before the great deportations of kulaks from the countryside, which was one of the features most closely associated with collectivisation.

Ironically, at the same time as this peasant discontent, Russian agriculture between 1925 and 1928 showed considerable growth:

- In some areas, for example Vologda province, land under cultivation increased by more than 25 per cent, and herds of cattle and horses by almost a third.
- Increasing prosperity put more peasants into the kulak bracket.

However, in contrast to this prosperity, State farms were much less efficient, less well run, and usually ran at a loss. The Communists knew this, despite their propaganda about the superiority of State enterprises.

It was this situation that led to the procurement crisis of 1928. For the previous years there had been increasing confrontations between peasants, particularly the prosperous kulaks on the one side and the party on the other. The party stepped up its propaganda against the kulaks, depicting them as a danger to society. Thus, there was already a class war in the countryside *before* collectivisation. One leaflet found in the mid-1920s declared:

> During the so-called target grain collection [i.e. War Communism] a robbery unheard of in history, a wave of peasant resistance threatened to overthrow the Bolshevik dictatorship. But the sly swindler Lenin, who has kicked the bucket thank God, managed to deceive the people by a manoeuvre of trickery. The robbery of grain requisitioning was replaced with the robbery by tax. The hope that the Bolsheviks will change their economic policy is nothing but the ravings of a madman. They intend to create on the bones of millions something impossible to create-Communism.

3　　　　　　　　　　*From a leaflet about grain collection in mid-1920s*

Fig. 4 *Political poster by Vladimir Mayakovsky (1893–1930): 'If you want something, join us. 1. You want to conquer cold. 2. You want to conquer famine. 3. You want to eat. 4. You want to drink. Quickly, join the brigade', 1921*

In this context, Stalin's policies had a certain logic. For Stalin, collectivisation would have to go hand in hand with industrialisation if the USSR were to become a great economic power. However, there was much more to it than a straightforward economic argument. Stalin and the rest of the regime knew that they simply did not control the hearts and minds, let alone the actions, of the mass of the Soviet population that just happened to live in the countryside. Therefore the regime could not feel at ease with its own population, even leaving aside its concerns about a hostile outside world. The fact that private enterprise in the countryside produced better practical results than State farming was subordinated to the political needs of the USSR as determined by Stalin and his party colleagues. This was possible once Bukharin and the right, which wanted more lenient treatment of the peasantry, had been defeated. Stalin was only reflecting what many ordinary party members thought, as in this complaint by a former member of the secret police to Victor Serge, a fellow Communist:

> Figures on unemployment, low wages, the seizure of the home market by private businessmen; deprivation in the villages and the creation of a peasant middle class; wretchedness in the cities and the arrogance of the newly rich – do these results seem natural to you? Have we done all that we have done, just for this? We did not fight the Revolution for this.

4 *Extract of a letter to Victor Serge from a former member of the secret police*

Activity

Source analysis

Study Sources 3 and 4: one was written by a Communist, one by a non-Communist. What do the have in common?

Industry

Industrial production in Russia had slumped during the Civil War and the period of War Communism. The introduction of the NEP in March 1921 did not lead immediately to a drastic change in industrial organisation, since most industry remained nationalised. However, although there was now internal peace, it was still a difficult time. State-run enterprises did not adjust easily to the new economic order of the 1920s. A money-based economy was introduced after 1921. However, this did not help the many enterprises that were inefficient and over-bureaucratic. As these enterprises lost money, production was cut and workers were often laid off. Therefore, although workers had the right to bargain for wage rises, there were frequent complaints about their wages and the privileges enjoyed by the party bosses. There were many strikes in the early 1920s, despite the sometimes strong action taken against strikers by the GPU. The party was not strongly represented in many factories, and many workers were reported as being unenthusiastic about the regime rather than being persuaded into believing that they were part of a blossoming new economic and social order. Workers from the Putilov factory in Leningrad wrote in a letter:

> As to how the unemployed live, it is hard to describe: they are hungry, ragged – their poverty knows no limit, their children sit in the street, right on the snow, for days on end, with their knees bare, because of holes, begging for a kopeck for bread. There is no one who gives: workers don't have much, the bourgeoisie look at them with disgust, and the commissars just ride by in automobiles. They don't care; they enjoy life.

5 *Extract of a letter by workers of the Putilov factory in Leningrad*

The situation did improve to some extent by the mid-1920s, although industry did not recover as quickly as agriculture. Industrial production

Fig. 5 *Poster about industrial strength in Soviet Russia c.1920s. 'Smoke from chimneys is the breath of Soviet Russia'*

■ Cross-reference

For more on the Shakhty trial, see page 85.

rose considerably compared to 1921, but in many cases it was still not up to 1913 pre-war levels. In addition to workers often being demotivated, they were having to operate outdated machinery. Productivity fell behind rising costs of production, and the workers' mood was not improved by discontent over **shortages of housing**. Many of the criticisms that later came to be made of Stalin's Five Year Plans, when industry in the 1930s was all about producing quantity rather than good quality goods, were equally true of the NEP industry in the 1920s. In particular, management was more concerned with getting money from the State to cover losses rather than concentrating on producing high-quality goods. There was, in any case, little incentive to be efficient and profitable, since any profits made went to the State, not to the enterprise itself. In contrast, smaller-scale privately owned businesses did well, even though they often paid higher wages. Average wages in State-owned industries were actually up to 50 per cent lower than pre-war levels, particularly for unskilled workers.

The Communists tried to address the problems, although the measures were largely unsuccessful in their impact:

■ In 1926, the **Supreme Council of National Economy (VSNKh)** was created. State enterprises contributed to a fund run by this organisation, in order to create a system of funding based on mutual support. In practice, this meant that more profitable enterprises (e.g. textile factories) tended to subsidise less efficient industries – hardly a recipe for long-term growth. Inefficiency led to higher prices and shortages of consumer goods, which is one of the reasons why peasants increasingly hoarded food or grew less of it. It was not in their interest to sell large amounts, since money had less value to them than keeping the agricultural produce.

■ When the government realised the seriousness of the problem, in 1927 and 1928 there was a drive to increase efficiency. However, it was done crudely, with an increase in targets but no accompanying increase in wages – leading to strikes in some regions. Inflation also made things worse for ordinary people.

■ Strikes were particularly damaging, not just for the impact on production but because the industrial proletariat, or working class, was held up, along with the party, to be the vanguard of the drive towards Socialism. Instead of being good role models, workers increasingly showed their disillusionment. Strikes hit key industries such as mining and metal production. Workers boycotted factory committee elections and trade unions, and unemployed workers also protested, leading to many arrests. Workers sometimes found food in short supply and there were instances of physical attacks on Communists, managers, and the traditional scapegoat, Jews.

In response to these problems, the authorities did not blame their own policies but looked for scapegoats, particularly 'class enemies', 'bourgeois specialists' and 'saboteurs'. This led to some of the early purges, such as the Shakhty trial when a group of engineers was accused of sabotage.

This crisis in industry suggested that the market economy aspect of the NEP simply could not sit comfortably with State-owned industry. High production costs resulting from inefficient enterprises led to higher prices, so people could not or would not buy products. Inefficiency rather than high wages caused the crisis, and most workers showed themselves as apathetic or hostile to the regime. The authorities realised the dangers, and there was a general acceptance that the NEP was not working, either ideologically or practically. Therefore there was already pressure for change before Stalin implemented the Five Year Plans. The motives for the change

came not just from an ideological drive to promote industrialisation and thereby pave the way for Socialism, but from a practical recognition that the NEP simply was not meeting the USSR's immediate needs.

Models of socialist development

The debate about the future direction of the Soviet economy and society was basically a debate about how and when NEP Russia should be transformed by the party into Socialist Russia, because it was not going to occur of its own accord. Although opinions did change and views were modified during the 1920s, it is possible to broadly identify three possible models that were the subject of much debate and controversy in the 1920s:

The Bukharinite model

Bukharin's name is often associated with the idea of 'gradualism', that is the idea of keeping the peasants on the side of the regime and allowing market forces to operate and drive the economy forward. This meant encouraging the peasants to 'get rich' and create the wealth that would allow the USSR to industrialise from a position of strength, and without creating excessive disruption or popular discontent.

However, it is also important to emphasise that Bukharin and his supporters also believed in the importance of a **centrally-controlled, planned economy** run by the dictatorship of the proletariat (or the Communist Party). They also accepted that the USSR must focus on developing heavy industry before a socialist society could emerge. Consumer goods, the things ordinary people wanted to buy in the shops, would have to wait. Where Bukharin differed from the left was in his belief that voluntary activity should be encouraged alongside the work of the party, and in his encouragement of a strong consumer market. He believed that this would allow for industrial growth during the transition phase to Socialism. A mixed economy (that is, a combination of State control and free market forces) was the key. Encouraging the growth of a prosperous peasantry would increase the demand for consumer goods. This, in turn, would boost the State-run industrial sector, which would gradually displace the private sector that operated under the NEP. At the same time, poorer and middle-class peasants would be encouraged to cooperate and thereby gradually displace the kulaks, the richer peasants who were individualistic in their approach.

Bukharin was defeated in 1929 and his policies never came near to being implemented. Many historians and economists are doubtful whether they would have worked in any case. Bukharin was wildly optimistic in his belief that the State sector was more efficient than the private sector and would therefore naturally displace it over time. He was also optimistic in his faith in the notion of the peasants and urban workers being close allies, although in this he was following Lenin's basic belief in such an alliance (known as the *smychka*). Bukharin's idea that the transition to Socialism could be peaceful and evolutionary went against the grain for the many Communists who had lived through the intense struggle of the revolutionary and civil war period. They were intent on forging a new world and driving out all remnants of the old class-based society as quickly as possible. Bukharin's idea that planning should and could be flexible and realistic was probably fanciful, and his ideas sometimes appeared to be contradictory: for example he supported the idea that the influence of kulaks should be limited, but he was at the same time opposed to any notion of using force. Bukharin followed the official line that the victory of Socialism in the USSR must ultimately depend on successful revolutions elsewhere in the world. However, he believed that

■ Key term

Centrally-controlled, planned economy: this was the model that was adopted by the USSR to manage the economy in the 1930s and beyond. It meant that all key decisions on what was to be produced were made centrally, in Moscow, according to a series of plans that set production targets for every industry.

the peasants might be the force that made the transition to Socialism in other countries. Bukharin declared that the peasantry had entered history as a 'great liberating force' that 'would decide the whole struggle'. Yet, Bukharin's ideas did not take enough account of the fact that peasants were not socialist by nature, which Stalin and others appreciated. Apologists for Bukharin have suggested that his arguments represented an alternative to Stalinism, being a more liberal vision of Communism or 'Socialism with a human face'. However, whilst it may have been a more humane vision, it is debateable as to whether it would have met the USSR's needs as determined at the time.

The Trotskyite or 'left' model

Trotsky is often seen as the representative of those proposing rapid and forceful industrialisation, combined with class warfare in the countryside against the peasants. This in effect is what happened under Stalin after 1928, although Trotsky's ideas were more wide-ranging, since they were also combined with promoting world revolution. Until 1926, Trotsky largely agreed with Bukharin that the party must recognise the role of market forces during a gradual transition to Socialism, whilst the State industrial sector expanded. However, from 1926 onwards, Trotsky became more critical of this gradualist approach, and like Stalin was very critical of the actions of peasants who were prepared not to sell their produce on the market if the price was not right. Trotsky therefore became an advocate, like Stalin later, of exploiting the peasantry in order to force through industrialisation as quickly as possible. He maintained his belief in international revolution because he did not believe that Russia had the resources to industrialise by its own means, and Socialism in One Country would leave Russia dangerously underdeveloped as well as exposing it to the continued hostility of a capitalist world.

Some of Trotsky's biographers, like the Russian historian Volkogonov, have been critical of Trotsky's policies, which they believe actually pushed Stalin himself towards a more extremist path and inadvertently helped Stalin to power. Trotsky despised reformism, that is a gradualist approach, of the kind associated with Bukharin. When Trotsky criticised those:

> who want to turn our country onto the capitalist path and want to weaken the position of the working class and poorest peasants against the growing strength of the kulak, the Nepman and the bureaucrat

it could have been Stalin himself speaking.

The Stalinist model

Stalin's ideas emerged during the 1920s, through his debates with rivals for the leadership and in his theoretical writings. He argued, unlike Trotsky, that the USSR *did* have the resources to build Socialism in Russia alone, and in this sense he agreed with Bukharin. However, Stalin also accepted that to create Socialism in Russia alone would be dangerous in a hostile capitalist world – therefore the USSR should still be concerned with promoting proletarian revolution abroad for its long-term security. However, this should happen only *after* the complete victory of Socialism in Russia, something that Trotsky found difficult to accept. Stalin virtually turned the argument on its head, by asserting that what stopped Russia from becoming socialist was not any deficiencies in the USSR itself, but the fact that the USSR had to exist in a hostile world, which gave support to 'enemies of Socialism' inside Russia. This is why the USSR had to act quickly to strengthen itself. It was also one of the main reasons given for the terror of the 1930s, with Stalin advancing the argument that as the USSR advanced on the road to Socialism (which for Stalin meant class war against the peasantry and all-out industrialisation), so foreign enemies would become more desperate. They would use agents and saboteurs to damage Russia from within – and such treacherous internal forces could conveniently be identified with 'Trotskyites' or anyone whom Stalin wanted to be rid of. In 1929, Stalin declared that:

> The dying classes are resisting, not because they have become stronger than we are, but because Socialism is growing faster than they are... And precisely because they are becoming weaker, they feel that their last days are approaching and are compelled to resist with all the forces and all the means in their power.

This was similar to Trotsky's position. However, where Stalin disagreed with Trotsky was on permanent revolution, since Stalin believed such a policy would expose the USSR to unacceptable risks by concentrating on revolution abroad and inviting more hostility before building up Russia's own strength to defend itself.

Stalin's position was not necessarily unMarxist. Marx had never been very precise about how Socialism would be achieved, since most of Marx's efforts had gone into analysing the capitalist society of his day. It was also possible for Stalin, and anyone else for that matter, to find statements from Lenin to support his own arguments. What can be said with certainty about the Stalinist approach is that it was 'orthodox' in the sense that it was committed to the development of a modernised, centrally planned and industrialised society, which would create the basis for wealth and eventually the elimination of classes, as peasants and proletarians fused into one. The particular emphasis that Stalin added to this vision was the development of the idea that everything necessary to carry the USSR through the transition period from the NEP could be achieved within the USSR, provided it was carefully planned. This had particular implications such as the focus on developing heavy industry and collectivisation, since industrialisation could not take place without a secure supply of food from within Russia itself. It also meant a priority for defence. Forcing through change rapidly in the face of international hostility, whilst at the same time ignoring the Bukharinite emphasis on consensus (agreement) and peaceful transition, also had important political implications. Above all, it meant strengthening the role of the party and the leader, since this was the only way the USSR could achieve the necessary self-sufficiency quickly and outdo its neighbours. Although Marxist and Leninist slogans were freely used to justify the changes, Stalinist economics came to be as much about promoting Soviet patriotism and national development as about focusing on bringing about a world in which classes were a thing of the past and all people lived in peaceful and happy collaboration for the good of all.

Production under the NEP

Table 1 on page 38 gives some indication of Soviet economic performance under the NEP. The statistics have to be treated with caution, but they do show a comparison between 1913, just before the First World War, and 1928, shortly before the end of the NEP.

Estimates of national income in 1928 vary from 93 per cent to 119 per cent of the 1913 level (with Western estimates at the lower end, and Soviet estimates at the higher end). The gap in productivity per head of population and the gap in technological advances compared to western European and US economies worsened between 1913 and 1928. Foreign trade in 1928 was only one-third of the 1913 level (due mainly to a decline in grain exports from the USSR). Although industrial

Cross-reference

For details of the terror, see Chapters 7 and 8.

Exploring the detail

Marx

All Communists looked to Marx for inspiration. Marx analysed past societies, and developed the idea that all previous societies had been based on the dominance of one class over another. He believed that eventually there would be a Socialist and then Communist State that was not class-based. However, Marx was mainly analysing the capitalist society of his day in the mid-19th century. He said very little about the future Communist State. Therefore Marx's followers often disagreed with each other about what precisely Marx's message was.

Activity

Revision exercise

Summarise or list briefly the main differences between the models of economic development. In your opinion, which model best suited the USSR's needs at this time?

Activity

Thinking point

1 How do you think the statistics in Table 1 were gathered?

2 Are they reliable or useful as evidence about the NEP?

3 Do they tell us how successful the NEP actually was?

production did recover significantly in the first half of the 1920s, there were significant variations between particular industries. In particular, consumer goods such as food lagged behind heavy industry.

Table 1 *Comparison of the value of commodities in 1913 and 1928*

	1913	1928
Coal (million tonnes)	29.1	35.5
Oil (million tonnes)	9.2	11.6
Electric power (billion Kwh)	1.9	5.0
Quality steel (million tonnes)	0.04	0.09
Cement (million tonnes)	1.52	1.85
Machine tools (thousands)	1.5	2.0
Tractors (thousand 15 hp units)	0.0	1.8
Lorries (thousands)	0	0.7
Cotton fabrics (million linear metres)	2,582	2,678
Woollen fabrics (million linear metres)	105	101
Grain (value in million roubles at 1926–7 prices)	4,566	3,641
Livestock (value in million roubles at 1926–7 prices)	6,221	5,901

Stalin's motives in launching rapid economic change

Stalin was clearly aware of all the economic issues surrounding the NEP. However, he would also have been very aware of other aspects of NEP Russia, since the regime received regular reports from the security services and party representatives throughout the USSR about the activities and opinions of ordinary people. This was a significant factor in the decision taken in the later 1920s to launch the second revolution, the drive to collectivise and industrialise the USSR. What concerned the authorities was not just the economic situation in the country, but various aspects of society and how people reacted to the regime. In any case, economics could not be divorced from social and political factors. The goal of Socialism was not just about changing the Soviet economy. It was about progress towards a different society, one in which class differences were abolished and a new type of 'Socialist man' – or woman – would emerge. All aspects of life would be affected – family life, leisure, beliefs – entertainment – not just the way in which people earned a living. It was these considerations, as well as a desire to improve the economy, that drove Stalin and other Communists to implement the 'Great Turn' of 1928–9. Whilst it may have been Stalin who was the driving force behind change, he was also representing the views of many party members, who enthusiastically took up the challenge. Stalin was clear in 1928 (Source 6):

> We must transform the USSR from a weak agricultural country dependent on world capitalism, drive out the capitalist elements mercilessly and create the economic basis for the construction of a socialist society.

6   *Quoted in D. Evans, **Stalin's Russia**, 2005*

NEP society

NEP Russia was an uneasy mixture of State authoritarianism and personal freedom, with the party gradually whittling away at the latter, although with only partial success before the 1930s. The success was partial because in NEP Russia, the communist regime, although it had done away with other parties and free elections, still contained independent voices and organisations, for example in the arts. There was also still much popular scepticism about official policies, as seen earlier in this chapter. The party was not yet powerful enough to control every aspect of life. It was an authoritarian society, but not yet a **totalitarian** one, because the regime had not yet moulded the population into a mindset in which their thoughts as well as actions were determined by the State. This was to be the big change in Stalin's 1930s USSR, when the use of both propaganda and force, backed up by many more State resources, became much more pervasive and together effectively crushed all possibility of truly independent thought or action.

The party certainly stepped up its propaganda campaign and attempted to influence hearts and minds during the 1920s in various ways:

- The Agitation and Propaganda Department became steadily involved in monitoring activities in all aspects of social life, including schools, newspapers, publishing generally and all areas of the arts and media. **Agitprop** clamped down on the dissemination of material considered not politically correct (often labelled with such terms as 'Menshevik') whilst simultaneously promoting the official party line. The guidelines became ever more restrictive, but were not always followed. For example, foreign films, despite their 'bourgeois ideology', continued to be shown in Soviet cinemas because they were more popular with the masses than Soviet films and brought in more revenue.

- Party organisations increased in size and the scope of their activities. Particularly important was the **Komsomol** (the Party Youth Movement), but there was a host of other organisations such as the League of the Godless and several women's organisations. These engaged in a wide range of propaganda campaigns. One example was the promotion of various days of 'revolutionary celebration' designed to divert people's attention from traditional religious holidays.

- **Education** was strongly targeted. The Communists set up their own party schools, but also influenced what was taught in ordinary State schools throughout the country. Teachers considered unreliable were sacked. Entries to higher education were screened to ensure that only students from the 'right' class background were admitted.

- **Religion** was increasingly attacked as being a class weapon of the bourgeois classes, designed to hoodwink the masses into accepting their downtrodden status. There was propaganda in support of materialism, that is, a non-religious system of belief, rather than religious belief and also campaigns against priests, the destruction of sacred relics, the disruption of religious services, and attacks on Church property. The Komsomol often played a prominent part in these activities. Defence of the Orthodox Church was hindered by its own internal division between traditionalists and the so-called 'Living Church' group that was prepared to modernise and compromise with the new atheist regime.

The success of the communist attempts to control and alter society were mixed. Undoubtedly there were many people who were pressured into conforming, or who were more interested in the opportunities provided

Fig. 6 *Propaganda poster showing male and female labourers working on an anvil, symbolising forging the future of the nation. In the background are industrial buildings and people at work. At the foot of the anvil are the hammer and sickle, the emblems on the national flag*

Key term

Totalitarian: a term referring to a society or political system in which the government tries to control all aspects of people's lives, using a combination of force and propaganda, and involving control over minds as well as actions.

Exploring the detail

Orthodox Church

Although there were many different religions practised throughout the USSR, including Islam and Judaism as well as various Christian sects, the most important church in European Russia was the Russian Orthodox Church. It had been the Established Church and a staunch supporter of the tsarist regime, and therefore inevitably found things difficult after the Bolshevik Revolution. Nevertheless, the Orthodox Church had widespread support in rural areas.

Fig. 7 *Propaganda poster on the education of the peasants, c.1920*

Fig. 8 *D. Moor, Soviet propaganda poster campaign against religion, 1918–23*

by the NEP to make money than worrying about cultural clampdowns. Some communist propaganda signally failed to hit the target. Religious life, particularly amongst rural peasants, became if anything more active, as the party's own internal reports indicated. Petitions were organised to re-open closed churches or to build new ones, and religious believers even got themselves elected to local Soviets. In order to discourage religious observance, the Communists were forced into a much more rigorous campaign of repression in 1929, involving the destruction of many churches, a ban on the teaching of religion, and other strict laws. Even so, religious belief was not killed off.

Communist attempts to change cultural and social life were also hampered by backsliding amongst those enforcing the message. This was particularly the case with the Komsomol. Rapid expansion of this organisation in the 1920s brought its own problems. Many recruits, especially in rural areas, were unsuitable. This party report on Komsomol activities was typical:

> Virtually no cultural or political educational work was carried out. Pervasive drunkenness and hooliganism was prevalent.

There were many reports of Komsomol members insulting priests, organising drunken orgies and threatening citizens, so it is not surprising that in many areas the Komsomol was very unpopular. There was a much bigger turnover of membership in the Komsomol than in the party itself, and the biggest causes of expulsion included drunkenness and hooliganism.

Many Communists also expected that the existing morality would be overturned, since like religion, it was associated with pre-revolutionary class attitudes. Many young Communists rejected marriage as a bourgeois leftover, yet, despite the theoretical equality of the sexes, young people's attitudes towards women were often marked by a complete lack of respect. Many girls would not join the Komsomol, because it was renowned for being so sexist, and female Komsomol members were frequently reported as being victims of rape or other forms of mistreatment. By attacking traditional social conventions such as the family and marriage, the party unwittingly encouraged other anti-social activities that were much more unwelcome, such as attacks on Jews. To cap it all, the evidence of the party's own investigations suggested that large numbers of Soviet youth in NEP Russia were certainly not enthusiastic about the new regime, and in some cases were not just apathetic but hostile. Many young people showed a preference for drink, Western lifestyles, or even religion, and were deaf to the appeal of Communism as it was put across by the authorities. The Central Committee of the Komsomol declared in 1927 that far from being enthusiasic about a new society:

> Apathy, disillusionment and decadent attitudes are not only among the main body of youth, but among the leaders. And as a direct result we find a growth in drunkenness, hooliganism and suicide.

7   *From a declaration by the Central Committee of the Komsomol, 1927*

Apart from fundamental dissatisfaction with the state of the economy, it was yet another reason for the decision to end the NEP and embark upon a second revolution. It was not just the economy but people's attitudes that needed changing.

The NEP and Soviet Socialism

From 1921 onwards, but particularly from after Lenin's death in 1924, NEP Russia experienced a change of direction. This was initially forced by circumstances – the difficulties encountered as a result of civil war and disruption after the revolution – but was also given an ideological justification to make the compromise with Capitalism at least partly acceptable to Communists. The change involved compromises:

■ There was much less emphasis on internationalism (the idea of world revolution) and much more on the realities of change inside the USSR alone – although the language of **proletarian internationalism** still featured strongly in propaganda.

■ The initial focus on class warfare immediately after the revolution, with abolition of class differences and discrimination against the bourgeoisie, was replaced with a more inclusive approach to society that allowed people incentives and the possibility of progress at the expense of others. For example, although some Communists objected, it was possible to make money through activities such as gambling, or through being successful in business. Therefore Soviet society allowed for inequalities and hierachies that the party condemned as unacceptable exploitation when practised in capitalist countries. It was even accepted that 'bourgeois' specialists might be necessary to help build Socialism.

And yet, despite these apparent compromises, official communist-speak was still dominated by phrases and concepts such as 'the victory of the proletariat' and 'internationalism'. Also, Communists continued to believe in a very materialist philosophy: the idea that by changing the environment, it was possible to create a better human being in the shape of socialist man (and also woman, although this was given less prominence). Hence the propaganda and activities of the 1920s, operated through instruments such as Agitprop, the government organisation devoted to spreading propaganda, although the evidence outlined suggests that this had a limited impact. The party was anxious to maintain centralised control and discipline, which involved repression, centralisation and an attempt to silence **dissent**, because it was felt that the comparatively liberal attitude towards the economy and society in NEP Russia could have dangerous consequences unless there were strict political and ideological controls in place. This accounts for the ban on factions inside the Communist Party itself, as well as the suppression of dissent in society at large when the NEP was introduced in 1921. This compromise between relative cultural and economic freedom on the one hand and political authoritarianism on the other hand was always an uneasy one. The party claimed not to be autocratic, and tried to encourage mass participation, but only if it was controlled by the party and directed into the 'right' channels. This is where the difficulties began:

■ The party did not have enough resources, and the mass of the population was not enthusiastic enough, to ensure that its attempts to direct and formulate policy were widely accepted, particularly when many aspects of people's lives did not show the degree of improvement that people had been led to believe would occur.

■ It was not yet clear how major issues would be resolved – such as:

– What should be the correct balance between centralisation and allowing local and personal decision making?

Fig. 9 *A 1932 cartoon showing the Church swept aside by communist progress in the countryside. (Courtesy of John Laver)*

■ **Key terms**

Proletarian internationalism: a popular communist phrase, meaning that the working people of all countries had more in common with each other than with their own countries, which suppressed and exploited them. Therefore working people should be internationalist in outlook and welcome the idea of a worldwide revolution that would bring the working class to power everywhere.

Dissent: 'dissenters' was a word used to describe those people who did not subscribe to the 'official' views that were put about by the regime through propaganda, education and so on.

– What should be the balance between the interests of the Soviet people and those of the international proletariat?

– What was the balance between State control and individual liberty?

– What should be the balance between centralisation and decentralisation?

– If there were to be important developments, above all in the direction of a more socialist society and economy, should this be forced and speedy, or gradual and carried out with the consent of the people?

– How should the desired partnership between the rural peasants and the urban proletariat be cultivated?

All these issues were hotly debated. The issues were even more important when they were overlaid with very practical considerations:

- The USSR rapidly needed to become stronger and more self-sufficient both in industry and agriculture. Could this be achieved without a massive effort involving the use of force?

- The USSR needed to become militarily strong in a hostile world. This depended on having significantly more industrial power.

- Eventually a Socialist State must prove its worth not just by eliminating the injustices characteristic of capitalist societies, but showing that it could offer its citizens a better standard of life.

- Politicians like Stalin were attempting to show that they were the true heirs of the great Lenin and the right leaders to carry through the transformation.

Given all these practical and ideological considerations, it is scarcely surprising that commentators at the time, and historians since, have debated such issues as: the degree to which the NEP was socialist; the degree to which it was driven by ideological or practical considerations; the degree to which it was popular; and the degree to which it was successful. However, the main consideration by the late-1920s was not the merits or demerits of the NEP in itself, but what was the best way of moving ahead into a socialist world as defined by the political heavyweights of the moment, primarily Stalin.

A closer look

Five historical interpretations

There are broadly five interpretations of the NEP as an economic system:

1 One group of mainly Western historians believe that the NEP did have the potential to sustain long-term economic development. In other words, they broadly accepted Bukharin's arguments. Some, like James Millar, believed that the rate of industrialisation eventually reached in the 1930s could have been achieved under the NEP with more sensitive methods and without collectivisation. They argue, for example, that control of prices could have persuaded peasants to sell more of their produce.

2 Until the 1980s, the orthodox Soviet position was that the NEP could not work. Although it was a legitimate policy in the early

1920s, to help the economy recover, and it could even be given some ideological justification as representing a halfway house to Socialism, it could not in the long term lead to a successful industrial economy. Therefore, the Stalinist model was basically the right one to adopt. Typical of this intepretation is the following extract (Source 8):

Socialism could not be built on the basis of a backward economy. The constant threat of war on the part of the aggressive imperialist powers demanded the development of a powerful industry to make the country economically independent in the shortest possible time. That was the only way for the Soviet Union to strengthen its defence capability and thus protect the construction of socialism... The transition to socialist industrialisation was attended by a sharpening of the class struggle throughout the country. The capitalist elements, which were out to retain their hold on the economy, were showing increasing signs of a revival... The anti-Leninist factions within the party stepped up their activities. They advocated a slowdown in the rate of industrial development... Trotsky proposed a national economic development plan which, if adopted, would have turned the USSR into an agricultural and raw material appendage of the industrialised capitalist countries... Trotsky did not believe an alliance between the working class and the middle peasants in the construction of socialism was possible.

8   *Y. Kukushkin,* **History of the USSR***, 1981*

3   A group of older Western historians, notably E. H. Carr, and some modern Russian historians, also hold that the NEP could not work in the long term. They argued that factors such as technological backwardness and the unstable nature of both the internal and world market could not have brought the USSR forward without more drastic State intervention.

4   Many Russian economists believe that the level of State interference in the NEP, such as central control of prices, was too restrictive and did not allow the Soviet economy room to breathe and expand, especially when the conditions at the time were taken into account. The situation was worsened by the apparent inability of the State to allocate resources effectively.

5   Many other modern historians such as R. Davies take a position somewhere in between the others, arguing that the NEP did have some life left in it, and sensible policies could have led to a certain amount of industrial advance (Source 9).

...given sensible price policies, a moderate rate of expansion of both industry and agriculture could have continued. On the other hand, we do not believe that NEP was capable of sustaining much higher rates of industrialisation than those achieved on the eve of the First World War.

9   *R. Davies, M. Harrison, and S. Wheatcroft, (eds.),*
The Economic Transformation of the Soviet Union, 1913–1945, *1994*

 Activity

Talking point

When you have studied the five interpretations of the NEP, debate which you think is the most convincing. Decide how successful the NEP actually was.

Learning outcomes

Through your study of this section you should have become familiar with the key developments in NEP Russia following Lenin's death in 1924. You should be able to explain why there was a leadership struggle after 1924, and why Stalin had emerged victorious by 1929.

As well as the role of personal rivalry, you should also understand why there was such a prolonged debate about the future direction of the USSR. You will have gained a good understanding of the main features of the economy and society of NEP Russia, and why these created problems as well as opportunities. You should also have some understanding of the varying interpretations of what happened and why people acted in the way they did.

Finally, you will have some understanding of how this links with the radical transformation of the USSR under Stalin, as explained in later chapters.

AQA Examination-style questions

(a) Explain why the NEP was unpopular with many Communists in the 1920s USSR. *(12 marks)*

 In answering part a), it would be useful to define what the NEP actually was and how it came into being. Then you can establish the extent to which it was popular or unpopular with Communists. For good marks, your answer should be reasonably wide ranging, for example considering the NEP in political, ideological, economic and social terms. Remember to keep your answer focused: this answer is about communist attitudes, not the attitudes of the mass of the people who were not party members.

(b) 'Stalin launched his second revolution in 1929 to defeat his rivals for the Soviet leadership.' Explain why you agree or disagree with this view. *(24 marks)*

 Part b) is quite demanding. You need to examine all of Stalin's possible motives. Undoubtedly you must discuss Stalin's struggle with his rivals. However, you need to write a balanced answer, which means considering other possible motives. Did Stalin also have genuine economic concerns and other motives for what he did? To get high marks you need to make a well-supported judgement in terms of the question.

3 Planned industrialisation

In this chapter you will learn about:

- why the USSR embarked on a massive programme of industrialisation by the end of the 1920s

- why a planning mechanism was adopted to carry out the process.

Fig. 1 *Propaganda poster by Nikolai Kogout: 'We have destroyed the enemy with weapons, we'll earn our bread thanks to our work. Pull up your sleeves, comrades!'*

Activity

Source analysis

What does Source 1 tell us about Stalin's motives for industrialisation?

We are fifty or a hundred years behind the advanced countries. We must make good this distance in ten years. Either we do it, or we shall be crushed.

1 *From a speech by Stalin in February 1931*

■ The motives for planned industrialisation

The situation in 1917

Russia had an industrial base by 1914 but still had a long way to go to compete with some of its European rivals. The governments of late tsarist Russia were concerned that industry should be expanded, in the interests of strengthening the country and ensuring national security. For this reason, they had strongly encouraged industrial investment, partly in order to maintain the railway system and to ensure that the armed forces were well supplied. They also helped privately-owned industry by imposing duties on foreign imports, so as to reduce foreign competition. However, most of production, both agicultural and industrial, was in private hands, and production depended largely on the forces of supply and demand, as in most European countries. This was to be the most significant difference from the Stalinist economy after 1928.

In the period before the First World War, industrial production in Russia grew at a considerably faster rate than agricultural production. Nevertheless, Russia was still basically an agricultural country. Agriculture accounted for three-quarters of employment and over half of national income. There were danger signs. The economy was considerably dependent on government support and foreign investment. Development was uneven: by 1913 cotton textiles employed 20 per cent of all workers in large-scale industry (mostly women). Because the State encouraged heavy industry, particularly the production of iron, steel and fuel, this sector expanded more rapidly than the production of products such as household goods for the Russian people. Soviet historians regarded these contradictions as very significant. They argued that they produced tensions that would have led to a revolutionary situation even without the major problems brought about by the First World War.

Conditions in developing towns were poor and a possible source of worker unrest, particularly among unskilled workers in the larger cities like Moscow and St Petersburg. Certainly it was many of these people who were to join the Bolshevik Party in the months before the October Revolution in 1917. There were already growing signs of working-class discontent in Russian cities by 1914. The First World War made problems worse. The role of the State in Russia, as in other countries, was considerably increased by the war. For example, special agencies were created to regulate production and prices. Although

Fig. 2 *Propaganda poster of workers producing iron and steel, 1938*

these methods of economic planning and control were often not very effective, they were taken over and adapted by the Communists after the 1917 Revolution.

The Soviet economy, 1918–28

As seen on pages 28–9, the Soviet economy was devastated during the 1918–21 Civil War, and then recovered under the NEP. However, fundamental weaknesses remained and industrial production was not sufficient either to make the USSR an industrial nation nor to pave the way to Socialism. In countries such as Germany, Britain and the USA, the middle class had provided much of the drive for industrialisation in the 19th century. After 1917, there was no middle class in the USSR, and therefore the State had to spearhead the drive to industrialise. As also seen on page 38, Stalin's motives for industrialisation were both political and economic. But he was not following a personal policy. Many ordinary party members welcomed the prospect of a new struggle, an economic one that would lead to Socialism and complete the work begun in 1917. Only the Soviet State could force through rapid change: the country's infrastructure was too weak, experience was lacking and there were too few developed resources for extensive industrialisation to take place without the full weight of the State behind it.

Why the Five Year Plans?

As indicated in Chapter 2, the Communists were determined to industrialise the USSR. It was necessary to strengthen the country against potential hostile foreign powers that feared the new Communist State. Communists also believed that a socialist society, based on the power of the working class, was only possible if Russia first went through an industrial transformation. This would hopefully produce the wealth enabling the construction of a society that would provide a secure existence for the Soviet people, since in Marxist terms, all wealth would belong to the people instead of to capitalists who exploited ordinary people to line their own pockets.

However, the decision on how to industrialise was not a simple one. Sokolnikov, who was the Commissar or Minister of Finance in 1924 and 1925, believed that the State should concentrate for the time being on investing in agriculture. The hoped-for increase in grain production would allow for more grain exports which, in turn, would pay for imports of industrial machinery. This was to become Bukharin's strategy. Soviet economists were divided on whether this was the best way forward. There were other advisers to the government in the mid-1920s who took another line. They wanted more industrialisation, but believed that this could be paid for from existing State-owned industry. By making industry more efficient, and increasing labour productivity, money would be available for yet more investment in industry. A major flaw in this argument was that existing NEP heavy industry was simply not efficient enough to provide such a surplus of profits for investment. The debates continued, but then the shortage of grain deliveries in 1927–8 forced the government's hand and led to the more drastic solutions associated with forced collectivisation and industrial planning.

There had already been some initial attempts to increase industrialisation in 1926–7, which were not promising. A well-publicised case was that of the Kerch Metallurgical Factory in the Crimea. By 1928, the costs of constructing this factory had more than tripled, putting other ventures at risk. There were complaints from managers that the planning agencies were chaotic, leading to decisions to start projects in unsuitable areas or to unaccountably suddenly stop those projects already under way. Technology bought with valuable reserves of foreign currency often turned out to be unsuitable for the intended purpose. It was the government's attempts to find scapegoats for these disasters that led to the 1928 Shakhty trial. A group of engineers working in the Shakhty coal mines in the Donbas region were accused of sabotage and treason. The Central Committee declared that this incident showed 'new forms and new methods of bourgeois counter-revolution against proletarian dictatorship and against socialist industrialisation'.

 The Shakhty affair was significant because of the way it was manipulated by Stalin. He and his followers decided that, due to the way it was organised, industry was simply unwilling or unable to use existing resources effectively. They decided that what they called 'bourgeois' specialists could not be trusted in the drive for Socialism. These must be replaced by politically reliable Communists who would run industry in the way that the State wanted. Stalin criticised the management of the NEP industry as follows (Source 2):

> Some Communists do not yet properly understand the technique of production and have yet to learn the art of management. So they let old technicians and engineers – the experts – carry on production. You Communists do not interfere with the technique of the business, but while not interfering, you should study technique, study the art of management tirelessly in order to later on become true managers of production, true masters of the business.

 *Quoted in H. Kuromiya, **Stalin's Industrial Revolution**, 1990*

Stalin was now making his priorities very clear. In another speech, in May 1928, he called for the speeding up of industrialisation as a means of providing more technology for agriculture in order to improve agricultural efficiency. But even more significantly, Stalin declared for the emphasis to be on heavy industry (Source 3):

> Should we, perhaps, for the sake of greater 'caution', hold back the development of heavy industry so as to make light industry, which produces chiefly for the peasant market, the basis of our industry? Not under any circumstances! That would be suicidal. It would mean transforming our country into an off-shoot of the world capitalist economic system.

3 *Adapted from a speech by Stalin, given in May 1928*

Stalin's industrialisation drive, begun in 1928, was directed by Gosplan, the State Planning Commission. The Communists made an early decision to base industrialisation on a series of Five Year Plans. This was a new concept, at least in peacetime. The government would determine what should be produced, and when, during a five-year period. Regional party leaders competed to put forward ambitious projects and argue with the authorities why their region should have first call on resources.

Activity

Revision exercise

Summarise why the method of industrialisation was a subject of keen debate in the 1920s USSR.

Activity

Thinking point

Why was the Shakhty affair significant in the decision to industrialise the USSR?

Activity

Source analysis

What do Stalin's speeches tell us about his attitude towards industrialisation and how it should proceed?

The plans would replace the existing mechanism that allowed the market, that is what ordinary people actually needed, to determine economic priorities. The Communist State justified its prominent role because it claimed to be representing ordinary people's interests rather than the interests of a privileged minority, as in the past. The language of class warfare become more and more strident as the industrialisation programme started, due mainly to Stalin and his supporters. Thousands of State employees were dismissed, including members of the planning offices, on the grounds that they were not sufficiently class-conscious, enthusiastic or free from corruption. However, Stalin was equally suspicious of party members, at a time long before the Great Terror of the mid-1930s. Already, in May 1928, he told a Komsomol audience (Source 4):

> Bureaucracy is one of the worst enemies of our progress. It exists in all our organisations – party, Komsomol, trade unions, and industrial management. The trouble is that it is not a matter of the old bureaucrats. Comrades, it is a matter of the new bureaucrats, bureaucrats who sympathise with the Soviet government, and finally, Communist bureaucrats. The Communist bureaucrat is the most dangerous type of bureaucrat. Why? Because he masks his bureaucracy with the title of party member. And, unfortunately, we have quite a number of such Communist bureaucrats.

 4   *From a speech by Stalin, given to a Komsomol audience, May 1928*

Highlighting class conflict as an important part of industrialisation meant more purging. For example, in the Donbas region, over half of all engineers and technicians had been arrested by 1931.

> To slacken the tempo would mean falling behind. And those who fall behind get beaten.... But we refuse to be beaten. One feature of the history of old Russia was the continual beatings she suffered because of her backwardness... her military backwardness, cultural backwardness, political backwardness, industrial backwardness, agricultural backwardness... Do you want our socialist fatherland to be beaten and to lose its independence? If you do not want this, you must put an end to its backwardness in the shortest possible time and develop a genuine Bolshevik tempo in building up its socialist economy. There is no other way. That is why Lenin said on the eve of the October Revolution: 'Either perish, or overtake and outstrip the advanced capitalist countries.'

5   *From a speech by Stalin in 1931*

> **Activity**
>
> **Source analysis**
>
> 1 What reason does Stalin give in Source 5 for rapid industrialisation?
>
> 2 What techniques does Stalin use to get his point across?

Preparations for a long-term plan had already begun in June 1927, although some major developments such as the Dnieper Dam and the Turksib Railway were begun even before this. A Five Year Plan was approved by the 16th Party Congress in April 1929, although the plan was then backdated to October 1928.

Two versions of the plan were presented to the Congress, which adopted the more ambitious of the two. This plan was not based on very secure data and was extremely over-ambitious. However, this did not stop targets being later adjusted upwards, in December 1929, when it was decided that the plan should be completed in four years. Any expert who urged caution or gave unwelcome advice to the political leadership was either ignored or denounced by Stalin, who by now was effectively the leader.

The main differences between the first three plans were as follows:

■ **The First Five Year Plan 1928–32** (which should have been completed in September 1933, but was deemed to have been completed in December 1932, making it a four-year plan) focused on the development of heavy industries (sometimes called producers' goods or capital goods) such as coal and steel – things not designed for their own sake, but as a means of making other products.

■ **The Second Five Year Plan 1933–7** was built on the infrastucture provided by the first plan. It gave more attention to consumer goods (things that people wanted to buy in the shops) than the first plan, but heavy industry remained the overall priority.

■ **The Third Five Year Plan**, begun in 1938, but disrupted by war in 1941, had a particular focus on the needs of the defence sector, in light of the growing threat that Nazi Germany posed to the USSR.

It was these plans that determined the basic economic structure of the USSR, a structure that lasted, with occasional modifications, until long after Stalin's death and right up to the break-up of the USSR in 1991.

The Soviet *Dictionary of Political Economy* defined the principles and practice of long-term planning in great detail. Source 6 shows an edited version.

The basic form of planning, the main instrument for carrying out the economic policy of the Communist Party, is the five-year plan. It relies on a system of scientifically-grounded technical and economic norms and standards governing the types of work, expenditures of labour, raw and other materials, fuel and energy, as well as standards for production capacity and capital investment based on economic and technical calculations. Annual assignments make plans more concrete: this ensures the unity of long-term and current planning. Long-term plans are major landmarks in creating material, technical, social and intellectual foundations ensuring transition to complete communism. Proceeding from the long-term socio-economic tasks determined by the Party, the USSR State Planning Committee and the relevant bodies work out draft guidelines for economic and social development which stipulate how major economic and social questions are to be dealt with. Once the five-year plan is adopted, it acquires the force of law. This way of compiling plans makes it possible, on the one hand, to manage the economy in a centralised way, and on the other, to develop the broad initiative of the working people and local economic management bodies; that is, to carry out the principle of democratic centralism in economic management.

 6

*Adapted from **A Dictionary of Political Economy**, 1981*

A Soviet school textbook summed up the ideas behind the Five Year Plans more simply (Source 7):

Simply restoring the economy of old Russia was not enough. The Russian Empire had no factories capable of making motor vehicles, tractors, aircraft and complex machine tools. For the Soviet Union to become an advanced industrial power it was necessary to build new mines and many metallurgical, chemical, tractor and engineering plants, to erect big power stations, to lay new roads, and to mechanise agriculture. Finally, it was necessary to produce tanks, aircraft and guns to make the Red Army strong and always able to repulse any enemy attack.

To build socialism the Communist Party and Soviet Government drafted five-year plans. The Soviet people were to transform a once backward Russia into an advanced industrial power completely on their own. No help could be expected from anywhere. The Soviet Union was surrounded by hostile capitalist states.

The entire country was transformed into one huge construction site. Everyone threw himself into the job of carrying out the five-year plan. The newspapers reported what was going on at the various building sites as if they were reporting from a battlefield.

The Soviet people had to deny themselves everything in order to buy foreign machinery at great cost and hire the services of foreign experts. People abroad believed it would take years and years before the Soviet Union would have an advanced industry. They did not know then what a free people building socialism could do.

7   *From a Soviet school text book*

Activity

Thinking point

Read Source 7. How much information is accurate and how much is propaganda or exaggeration?

Summary questions

1 Explain why the Communists believed that industrialisation was an important priority for the USSR.

2 Explain why economic plans were considered the best way to move industrialisation forward.

4   The impact of industrialisation to 1941

In this chapter you will learn about:

- the main features of the first three Five Year Plans

- the successes and failures of these plans

- the impact industrialisation had on the USSR's economy and society.

Activity

Source analysis

Can you explain the humour in the jokes given in Source 1?

The speaker at a meeting is talking on the theme of: 'We will catch the capitalist countries.'

One of the audience asks: 'When we catch them, can we stay there?'

Question: What would happen if you built Communism in the Sahara desert?

Answer: Everything would be fine for the first three years, but then there would be a serious shortage of sand.

A Muscovite walks into a shop with empty shelves.

'Hmm. I see you have no bread,' the disappointed shopper murmers.

'You're wrong, comrade,' the shop assistant declares. 'We sell fish here. And we have no fish. The store that has no bread is in the next street.'

---

1   *Soviet jokes from the 1930s*

The successes and failures of the first three Five Year Plans, 1928–41

The basic differences between the first three Five Year Plans were outlined on page 50. The plans determined the course of the Soviet economy from 1928 to the German invasion in 1941, when the plans' achievements were severely put to the test.

A closer look

An overview of the plans

The economic historian R. Davies (*Soviet Economic Development From Lenin to Khrushchev*, 1994) subdivided the period of the plans into five key periods, taking into account the changes in agriculture that accompanied industrialisation, and giving an overview of overall economic performance:

1928–30 Heavy industry expanded at an accelerating pace, with increasingly ambitious targets. Collectivisation was occuring at the same time. The labour force rapidly expanded during this period.

1930–2 Expansion was constricted as the USSR struggled to meet the over-ambitious targets. Industrial production slowed, and there was also a temporary halt to collectivisation. The government adopted a slightly more realistic and less fervent approach to expansion.

1933 Whilst famine gripped large areas of the USSR, the 1933 industrial plan was more modest and realistic. Priority was to be given to completing projects begun during the first Five Year Plan.

1934–6 Economic development was spectacular – many new factories came into operation, whilst agriculture began to recover. Labour productivity and the standard of living improved, with consumer rationing abolished in 1935.

1937–41 Economic policy was geared to rearmament, but was affected adversely by the terror. People now had more money to spend, but less on which to spend it.

The First Five Year Plan, 1928–32

Partly because good progress was made during the first phase of the plan's implementation, the targets were adjusted upwards in December 1929, with calls to fulfil the plan ahead of schedule. Stalin was insistent:

> We must increase the tempo... We are fifty or a hundred years behind the advanced countries. We must make good this distance in ten years. Either we do so, or we shall be crushed.

The emphasis was therefore not so much on building Socialism but on strengthening Soviet national defences against a hostile invasion.

The following were the key features of the first plan:

- There were several huge projects, for example the construction of Magnitogorsk. This was a steel-producing city, built from nothing mainly by enthusiastic young Communists.
- Resources were targeted on heavy industry. Small-scale industry such as handicrafts and enterprises catering for domestic goods for the home were starved of resources and declined.
- The priorities within the plan meant that consumers' needs were neglected. For example, it was often very difficult in the 1930s to buy a pair of shoes – simply not enough were made nor distributed.
- There were impressive gains in several areas of heavy industry, for example engineering. However, not all targets were met, for example in steel and chemicals production. Textile production fell because of a shortage of resources.
- Problems were caused by gaps in the infrastructure. For example, road and rail transport were inadequate to meet the demands of industry. Transport and housing were also inadequate to cope with the increase in numbers of town dwellers.
- There was a rapid increase in urbanisation, not just in European Russia, including Moscow and Leningrad, but also beyond the Urals and in some other republics.
- Whereas under the NEP there had been unemployment, there was now a shortage of labour, despite an increase in the length of the working week in 1931. Many of the new workers were inexperienced peasants. There were too few specialists such as engineers, and the gaps were only partly filled by recruiting specialists and skilled workers from abroad.
- The workforce changed in character, partly through the large numbers of convicts and women (especially the latter) added to the workforce.

Fig. 1 *Propaganda poster by Victor Deni and Nikolai Dolgorukov, 1933, celebrating the Soviet success in completing the First Five Year Plan in four years, and thereby turning the tables on the capitalist enemies who scoffed at the plan in 1928*

Fig. 2 *Magnitogorsk complex, on a morning during the First Five Year Plan*

■ Wages rose, as managers of enterprises sought the labour they desperately needed to fulfil the plan targets. However, there were too few goods on which to spend money. Therefore, initially, there was rationing of goods such as clothes and food in cities, and prices were fixed by the State. In reality, regulations were often ignored, so that prices did rise rapidly, especially in private food markets. The government paid peasants low prices for their produce.

■ Although industry and agriculture were linked, there was always an assumption by the Communists that industrial interests took precedence over agricultural ones: agriculture was expected to provide raw materials for industry; workers for expanding industry; food for the urban workforce; and exports to pay for industrial imports.

Activity

Thinking point

Answer these questions based on the statistics in Table 1.

1. Summarise the difference between the two versions of the First Five Year Plan.

2. Which industries were expected to make the greatest rate of progress during the plan, and which the least?

3. What questions might you ask about the reliability of these statistics and how they were compiled?

4. Do these statistics suggest that the plan was a success? What else would you need to know?

Table 1 *Targets for industrial output during the First Five Year Plan*

Output targets	1927–8 actual production	1932–3 first version	1932–3 'optimal' version
Coal (million tonnes)	35.4	68	75
Oil (million tonnes)	11.7	19	22
Steel (million tonnes)	4	8.3	10.4
Iron ore (million tonnes)	5.7	15	19
Pig iron (million tonnes)	3.3	8	10
Electricity (milliard Kwh)	5.05	17	22
Machinery (million roubles)	1822	?	4688

*Soviet statistics adapted from A. Nove, **An Economic History of the USSR**, 1969*

When the plan was drafted in 1929, there were two versions. The 'optimal' version of the plan was the more ambitious version, which was eventually adopted.

The plan certainly did not run smoothly, for several reasons. It should first be emphasised that there was never one coherent plan. In fact, it was not really a 'plan' at all, since it was not a carefully thought out programme, with no clear objectives, no cost analysis and no realistically targeted resources.

When resources were allocated to a particular sector, the possible impact of that decision on other sectors was often ignored. The plan was largely a set of crude targets and exhortations, with little attention to the difficulties that might be encountered. The government adapted the plan as it went along, increasingly tightening its grip but not actually making the economy more efficient. Although there were specialists with some knowledge and experience, they often found themselves in conflict either with Communists, who were full of zeal but had no appreciation of realities, or with desperate administrators simply concerned to meet their particular targets.

The government became aware of the problems, but instead of going back to basics it adopted a 'carrot and stick' approach to production by simultaneously coercing workers and 'bribing' them with incentives. On the one hand, there was a strict approach to labour discipline, for example with absenteeism punished, and an increase in taxes. However, on the other hand, workers in important industries were given higher wages as an inducement to greater effort. At a strategic level, in order to keep up production, the government got financial credits from abroad and exported wheat so as to be able to buy foreign machinery and expertise, despite shortages at home amongst the Soviet population.

The great experiment

Whilst it is easy to criticise the imperfections in the plan model, it should be emphasised that the First Five Year Plan was a great experiment, and there was no obvious blueprint or real example elsewhere from which to learn. As one economic historian put it (Source 2):

Fig. 3 *Propaganda poster by A. Deineka: 'Mechanisation of the Donbass', 1930*

> Russia was growing, the western capitalist system was apparently collapsing [during the Great World Depression beginning in 1929], with massive unemployment and social disruption, culminating in America with the paralysis of 1932–3, in Germany with six million unemployed and the triumph of Hitler. The worst period of Russia's own crisis coincided with crashes and bankruptcies in the 'capitalist' world, and at least Russia's troubles could be seen as growing pains… The West was no sort of model for Russia or anyone else to follow.

2	
	*A. Nove, **An Economic History of the USSR**, 1969*

Activity

Research exercise

Individually or in groups, research the causes of the Great Depression that began in 1929. Why did the USSR not suffer the same effects as other Great Powers such as the USA, Germany or Britain?

If the Soviet strategy is to be blamed, perhaps it is for the fact that many of the imperfections of the plan were not adequately analysed and put right, because people were afraid to tinker with it as Stalin's regime became more authoritarian. In this climate any criticism might easily be labelled as disloyalty, sabotage or treason. Therefore potential critics buried their heads in the sand. It was even worse for the USSR in the long run that faults in the initial plan, such as ignoring the importance of quality in favour of sheer quantity, were firmly embedded in Soviet political and economic culture. This meant that Soviet economic performance was undermined for the next 50 years, and even the successes that were achieved came at enormous cost and put an eventually disastrous strain on the system.

The Second Five Year Plan, 1933–7

Fig. 4 *1929 Soviet poster showing opponents of the Five Year Plan (the Capitalist, the drunkard, the priest, the white general, the lying journalist, etc.) (Courtesy of John Laver)*

There were some improvements made to the second plan, which was adopted by the 17th Party Congress in February 1934. The plan was much better prepared than the first, whilst its organisation was less chaotic and also less ambitious. This was partly because when it was drafted in 1933, the USSR was in crisis, suffering from a horrendous famine, shortages and a decline in investment and production. Therefore there was more realism in the planning, and the benefits were seen in considerable industrial progress made during the plan's implementation.

The successes were also due to the fact that the USSR began to benefit from the improving infrastructure that had been laid down, at great cost, during the first plan. For example, the new 'steel city' of Magnitogorsk only came into full production during the second plan. There were now big gains in industry, construction and transport. Consumer goods received more attention, and they were actually targeted for a greater share of investment than heavy industry. Some consumer goods, such as gramophones, made virtually their first appearance in the USSR as far as ordinary citizens were concerned. Productivity and wages both rose, whilst prices fell. Even so, the targets still proved too optimistic and were not met, particularly in consumer goods and housing. The plan also did not meet the aim of higher real wages (that is, what incomes were actually worth when prices were balanced against money wages). The failures were largely due to the higher priority increasingly given to defence, where output rose by almost 300 per cent between 1933 and 1938. Every industrial complex contained at least one secret workshop devoted to weapons production.

This secret output did not appear in the published military budget, even though it may have provided almost half of Soviet military production.

Although the output of machinery and the generation of electricity, coal and rail transport did not meet all the targets, there were nevertheless impressive advances in these areas. The USSR was also able to survive with fewer imports such as machine tools.

Workers now had more incentives than fear to drive them on. Rationing was abolished, and there were more goods to buy, even if the quality was not always good. Many workers were now more experienced and better educated or trained. Possibly for these reasons productivity rose, in addition to the efforts of those driven on by propaganda incentives like the Stakhanovite movement. However, although

Fig. 5 *Congress of the Communist Party. Kirov surrounded by the dignitaries of the Soviet Union (Joseph Stalin, second from left), 1934*

workers probably felt better off, life was still hard: labour discipline remained strict, with an increase of between 10 and 50 per cent in labour norms by 1936. These norms were production targets that workers were expected to at least meet or, even better, to exceed. Failure to meet the norms could result in fines or more serious punishments. The gap between workers' wages and those of better-paid professionals widened. Apart from the danger of an 'unsatisfactory' worker disappearing as a purge victim, crimes such as absenteeism could lead to dismissal or the loss of allocated housing space.

A closer look

The Stakhanovite movement

Alexei Stakhanov was a coal miner in the Don basin. On 30 August 1935, he did a five-hour shift, cutting 102 tonnes of coal with his pneumatic pick. This was 16 times the average for a shift. He was immediately hailed as a Soviet hero and given a large bonus and many other material benefits and honorary awards. Propaganda magnified Stakhanov's status and the idea of forming 'Stakhanov groups' in an attempt to achieve similar feats or to set new records caught on. It was ideal propaganda for a society trying to create a new civilisation based on teamwork and selfless sacrifice.

Many years later, it was revealed how much of Stakhanov's feat had been just that, a propaganda stunt. For the famous shift, Stakhanov had been given a support team of several workers who had done everything possible to support him, carrying out a range of tasks that all miners were normally expected to do for themselves, such as propping up the roof. This enabled Stakhanov to focus exclusively on cutting coal.

The Stakhanovite movement was not popular with many workers at the time. There are records of Stakhanovites being victimised or even attacked by colleagues who were less enthusiastic and resented campaigns to persuade them to work even harder.

Towards the end of the plan, investment and production fell away. This was partly due to the increasing emphasis on defence prodction, but also due to the growing impact of the terror. The terror hit groups such as managers and specialists disproportionately highly, which meant the loss of many experienced and skilful people. It also increased the reluctance of those with responsibility to be innovative, since any perceived failure would not be excused, but could easily result in arrest or worse.

The Third Five Year Plan, 1938–41

The Third Five Year Plan was prepared during 1937–8, although not formally adopted by the 18th Party Congress until March 1939. It had ambitious targets: for example a 92 per cent rise in industrial production over five years. It also promised to expand the provision of secondary education throughout the USSR.

However, the approach of war changed priorities and the original targets could not be met. There were also specific stumbling blocks that had a serious impact, notably a shortage of skilled labour and a shortage of oil, which amounted to a crisis. Some relief was gained by the Soviet occupation

Exploring the detail

Soviet expansionism

In 1939, the USSR occupied eastern Poland and in 1940 the three Baltic States of Latvia, Estonia and Lithuania. This was under the terms of a treaty with Germany, although the main purpose of the occupations was to increase Soviet border security against a possible German attack.

of eastern Poland in late-1939, and the Baltic States in 1940, which added to the USSR's economic potential.

The working of the plans – the Stalinist command model

Fig. 6 *Anonymous propaganda poster: 'Let us accomplish the Five Year Plan within four years. Let us go forward to achieve this goal', 1930*

The USSR's economy in the 1930s, and for many years afterwards, was a very top-down model, in other words, virtually all the decisions about planning were made at a high level. Very few, usually very small, private enterprises remained outside State control in the 1930s, and they were often starved of resources. State-run industrial enterprises got their orders from the centre. There was no negotiation: enterprises were bound to carry out the plan, which set out details of specified output, prices, the wages of employees and so on. **Gosplan** coordinated the plan at the centre. Each Five Year Plan was broken down into yearly operational plans and sometimes even quarterly targets. Gosplan's political bosses decided what the national economic or political priorities were during the planning stage. These priorities then determined what was to be produced, without any regard to other important factors such as what consumers might want, or considerations of profit and loss. The bureaucracy was eventually made up of 20 ministries or People's Commissariats, the largest of which was responsible for heavy industry. It was run by Ordzhonikidze between 1930 and 1937. The other three major Commissariats covered light industry, food and timber. These organisations gave orders directly to enterprises, directing them not just about quantities to produce but where the enterprise should purchase resources, what wages it should pay, and what prices it should charge. There was another layer of bureaucracy provided by regional administrators, who issued instructions or decided on how resources should be allocated across all industries in a particular region or even in a republic. Therefore the responsibilities of regional and ministerial organisations often cut across each other, which was not a very efficient system.

The impact of the terror on the economy

Cross-reference

For more information on the terror, see Chapters 7 and 8.

The administration of the economy was one of the first areas of the USSR to experience the results of Stalinist purges. Stalin and his followers automatically assumed that many of the old officials and experts who manned the bureaucracy were politically unreliable and might even be sabotaging policies such as rapid industrialisation. Therefore, in the late-1920s and early 1930s, large numbers of officials were investigated and removed. Some of those removed were classified as 'enemies of Soviet power', which was 'Category 1' and therefore amongst the most serious of offences. Hundreds of officials were removed from Gosplan, VSNKh, and the Commissariats [ministries]. Twelve thousand workers were promoted into their places. The Central Statistical Administration was closed in 1929. Gosplan took over its activities, so that statistics were firmly subordinated to what suited the planners. Over half of trade union leaders and factory committees were replaced.

Managers did not have to worry too much about trade unions, since these were virtually toothless. Trade unions performed some functions, such as looking after workers' welfare, but they were controlled by the party and would not challenge key decisions, and certainly not organise strikes. However, managerial initiative was stifled. Managers were afraid of making mistakes. There were contradictions in the way that enterprises were run. Stalin firmly believed in the principle of one-man management: the party and union representatives in factories were there to 'help' managers, for example in controlling workers, but were strictly forbidden from questioning managerial decisions. However, in practice, the political leadership frequently did put pressure on management. For example, in July 1940, a decree was issued making poor quality production a criminal offence, so that in theory at least, enterprises now had to worry about quality as well as meeting quantative targets. This interference breached a Central Committee directive of 1929 to the effect that enterprises such as factories should be managed by one person, free from interference by the party organisation, which would be represented in the enterprise.

Soviet citizens paid relatively little tax, since the State simply paid costs of production out of revenue gained from the sale of goods from its own enterprises.

Table 2 *Industrial production under the plans*

	1932	1937	1940
Coal (million tonnes)	64	128	166
Steel (million tonnes)	0.68	2.39	2.79
Cement (million tonnes)	3.48	5.45	5.68
Machine tools (thousands)	20	48	58
Oil (million tonnes)	21	28	31
Electric power (billion kwh)	13	36	48
Tractors (thousand 15 hp units)	51	66	66
Lorries (thousands)	24	180	136

From Russian sources, adapted from R. Davies, M. Harrison, and S. Wheatcroft, The Economic Transformation of the Soviet Union, 1913–1945, 1994

Activity

Thinking point

1 Reproduce the figures from Table 2 as a block graph or line graph.

2 What do these statistics tell us about the rate of industrial progress during the period of the first three plans?

3 Where are the gains most impressive?

4 What else would you want to know if you were trying to explain how successful or otherwise the plans were?

The impact of industrialisation on the Soviet economy to 1941

On one level at least, Stalin's industrialisation should be counted as a success. By 1941, the USSR had an industrial base that enabled it first to withstand the violent German assault in 1941 and then eventually to win the war, when this industrial power was combined with the heroic efforts of the Soviet people and other factors such as Stalin's leadership. What the Soviet economy could not do was sustain both a massive defence capability and a high standard of living at the same time (in marked contrast, for example, to the USA). This remained a problem for the USSR for the rest of its history.

When measuring success, we also have to bear in mind the difficulties of calculating growth, since Soviet statistics from the 1930s are unreliable and often deliberately falsified. The growth rates for foodstuffs and consumer goods were greatly exaggerated. For example, from 1933 onwards, grain output was measured by its 'biological yield': that is, its maximum possible yield as the grain stood ripe in the fields. No

Fig. 7 *At Magnitorgorsk, steel pigs being rolled through cylinders at the Stalin Iron Foundries, the heart of the Soviet steel industry in the Ural region, November 1941*

allowance was made in the calculations for the inevitable losses that would occur for example during harvesting, when there would be losses due to problems such as waste and transport difficulties.

Bearing these warnings in mind, it is possible to make some overall assertions:

■ The Soviet economy between 1928–40 probably grew at 5 to 6 per cent each year, an impressive result.

■ Many of the developments, such as several branches of engineering, were begun almost from nothing.

■ According to R. Davies, 'The armaments industry of the 1930s was the most outstanding success of the pre-war Soviet economy' (*The Economic Transformation of the Soviet Union*) – a significant claim, since a life or death struggle against Nazi Germany was on the horizon. Several aspects of Soviet weapons construction were almost entirely new, and some of the tanks, aircraft and guns produced were the equal of, and in some cases superior to, anything produced elsewhere in the world. Soviet defence production received increasing priority and was allocated the best raw materials.

■ There was a geographical shift in industry. Whereas before 1930 industry was sited mainly in north-west and central European Russia, after 1930 there was considerable investment in Siberia, the Urals and the previously undeveloped Central Asian republics.

■ There was a considerable population shift. Between 1926 and 1939, the urban population increased from 26 to 56 million people, with the increase mostly the result of large-scale migration from the countryside to the towns, where there was a higher standard of living.

■ There was a dramatic change in the nature of the workforce. In 1928, women made up 24 per cent of the workforce; this figure was up to 39 per cent by 1940. In 1931, there was the largest yearly increase in workers joining the industrial sector in Soviet history (26 per cent). Between 1928 and 1932, the industrial workforce doubled.

■ Although overall industrial production increased considerably, the quality of many products, especially consumer goods, was poor.

Socialism or Stalinism?

The USSR claimed to have achieved Socialism as a result of the 1930s industrialisation because, by the Soviet definition, Socialism meant 'social' ownership of the means of production. In other words, all people collectively 'owned' factories and shops, or rather the State did on people's behalf, so that there were no profits being made by some people at others' expense. The Soviets claimed that State ownership was just a particular form of 'social' ownership, since the State was protecting the individual against the exploitation of the citizen by profit-seeking capitalists, which was the hallmark of capitalist countries whose economies were based on private enterprise. The Soviets never claimed under Stalin to have achieved Communism, because to get to that far-off stage, the State with all its organising and governing bodies would have had to have 'withered away'. The Soviet case was based on the fact that even as early as 1929, less than one per cent of large-scale industry was in the private sector, and the few remaining private factories were closed in 1930. Those hostile to the USSR asserted that the USSR was not a Socialist State, because 'social' ownership under Stalin did not exist for the good of the people. Rather, it was a form of dictatorial or totalitarian power in which all activity, including economic activity, was determined by what the unelected leaders decided was good for the party and the State, without taking the needs of individual citizens into account.

Fig. 8 *Tricot factory installed in the convent Znamenski, 1930*

There has been a tendency by Western historians to treat industrialisation as essentially a drive for production and national strength. However, to Stalin and his followers, the ideological motive for industrialisation appears to have been equally important. Stalin promoted the industrialisation campaign as one of class warfare, and far from trying to unite the nation, deliberately split it, using committed groups like the Komsomol to preach war against 'class enemies' who were trying to hold up progress. Typical was Stalin's statement in 1933 that 'has-beens' or 'class enemies' had:

> wormed their way into our plants and factories, into our government and trade institutions, into our railway and water transport enterprises, and principally, into the collective farms and State farms.

Hence, as industrialisation continued, so did the purges.

The balance sheet of success and failure

Some of the regime's objectives were achieved, some not (Table 3).

Table 3

Successes	Failures
There was a rapid expansion of industrial production, mostly in areas of heavy industry such as coal and steel.	Not all targets were met, e.g. in the chemicals industry, through inefficiency, wastage, faulty decisions, etc.
There were some high-quality achievements, e.g. in defence production and in hydro-electric power.	Although quality did improve during the 1930s, many products remained of poor quality.
The USSR became almost self-sufficient in some areas such as machine tool production.	Targets for consumer goods production were not met.
There was some degree of industrial modernisation. The shifting of production to relatively 'new' areas like Central Asia was partially achieved.	

Interpretations

Virtually all historians and economists, whatever their nationality or own political persuasion, agree that the industrialisation of the USSR in the 1930s achieved some remarkable successes. What is at issue is chiefly

Activity

Group discussion

Based on the information in Table 3, construct a debate on this motion: 'The Soviet industrialisation programme in the 1930s was a major achievement and proved the wisdom of Stalin's policies.'

Exploring the detail

Destalinisation

Three years after Stalin's death in 1956, there was a campaign in the USSR known as Destalinisation. Some of his ex-colleagues began to denounce Stalin for the brutality of his rule and some of the mistakes he had made. However, leading party members blamed Stalin personally rather than themselves or others in the party. They still accepted that Stalin had been right to carry out the economic policies he did. Moreover, most of the systems set up in Stalin's time, including the system of economic planning, remained in place for many years after Stalin's death.

the debate about whether the successes outweighed the costs, or whether there could have been an alternative, less disruptive approach.

The orthodox Soviet position, even after Stalin was denounced for his personal excesses, from 1956 onwards, was to emphasise the basic correctness of Stalin's approach. The basic thrust of Soviet historiography was that (Source 3):

> Within an incredibly short space of time in historical terms the Soviet people led by the Communist Party successfully tackled such formidable tasks as the laying of the material and technical foundations of socialism, the creation of its socio-economic base, the transformation of the social and class structure of society, the solution of the national question and the rise in the material and cultural standards of Soviet people... Socialism had scored an ideological victory as well, since Marxism-Leninism became the dominant ideology in the country... Socialism was now a tangible reality.

3   *Y. Kukushkin,* **History of the USSR***, 1981*

Some economists (for example H. Hunter, (1973) *The Overambitious First Soviet Five-Year Plan*) accept that Stalin's methods resulted in significant gains in industrial production in a short space of time, even though 'impossible' targets could not be met. However, the argument goes that this model was not the only possible one. Alternatives might have avoided the terrible destruction and waste, the weakened agricultural sector and the accompanying terror if there had been a more gradualist and less-ambitious approach. In other words, many of the successes could have been achieved without the terrible by-products that were the hallmark of Stalinism. This line of argument is also shared by some historians like R. Tucker (*Stalin As Revolutionary*), supporting Bukharin's view that longer-term economic development could have risen out of the NEP without the dislocation of Stalin's methods. The main weakness of these arguments is that they tend to focus on the economic results but play down the political and social aspects, which were equally important to many Stalinists, who were obsessed with class war as much as growth. Other historians like A. Nove (*Was Stalin Really Necessary?*, 1962) have tended to dismiss the viability of some of these 'moderate' alternatives and have argued that there was a certain logic in Stalin's methods, given the backwardness of Russia: the argument that 'It is impossible to make omelettes without breaking eggs'.

M. Malia (*The Soviet Tragedy: a History of Socialism in Russia*, 1994) takes the view that Stalin had achieved his main objective by 1936, in that he had replaced the capitalist system of production characteristic of countries such as the USA and Britain. However, his argument is that the Soviet achievement was largely improvised and did not have any of the moral virtues which Socialism had traditionally preached, such as freedom, equality, an abundance of goods, and an end to exploitation. These did not happen because the Soviet experiment was carried out by an all-powerful State, and State power is almost always incompatible with values such as equality and freedom. Advocates of this line of argument tend to describe the Soviet system as 'State Capitalism', 'State Socialism' or simply 'Stalinism', rather than 'true' Socialism.

Any discussion of industrialisation is bound to be coloured by other aspects of Stalinism. It is impossible to evaluate Soviet industrialisation in isolation: it was bound up with other important factors affecting the political and social state of the USSR in the 1930s.

Activity

Revision exercise

Summarise the different interpretations of Stalin's industrialisation. Which do you find most convincing, and why?

■ The impact of industrialisation on Soviet society to 1941

Chapter 9, pages 113–127, contains an analysis of the impact of Stalinism on Soviet society. Here, there is a brief analysis of how industrial changes in particular affected Soviet citizens in the 1930s.

Peasants

Peasants were affected principally in two ways:

1   *Either* they remained as peasants, living in the countryside on collective or State farms. They worked hard, often in worse conditions than people in towns, and much of their produce was taken by the State. Those who also cultivated small private plots might do better, since they were allowed to consume the produce themselves or sell it in private markets.

2   *Or*, like the majority, they moved to the towns, voluntarily or because they were forced off the land during collectivisation. It was easy to find work because the factory workforce was rapidly expanding. However, the transition was not easy for most ex-peasants. They came from a different background where there was less emphasis on labour disciplines such as punctual time keeping. They were rarely used to handling machinery. They were not always enthusiastic and frequently changed jobs. However, they were hired because their labour was cheaper than the cost of skilled or semi-skilled workers. But as a rule, untrained peasants did not boost the level of productivity.

Workers

Workers' attitudes varied. Many had been unenthusiastic about their conditions under the NEP and welcomed the prospect or the promise of better conditions. Many younger workers, particularly if they were party members, were very enthusiastic about the industrialisation drive, since it seemed to give a meaning to what might be very boring work. Many volunteers flocked to projects such as the building of Magnitogorsk. Some workers benefited from better education and the initial reaction against 'bourgeois' specialists. It gave them the opportunity for rapid promotion, and some became managers. Many experienced a rise in the standard of living, especially when working and living conditions improved. Skilled workers were in high demand and were comparatively well paid, especially if they stayed in their jobs. They might receive special perks such as access to special food shops or better housing. After 1931, paying different workers different rates of pay was permitted, and higher productivity could lead to bonuses.

On the other hand, less enthusiastic workers suffered. Absenteeism was punished and there were other tough measures of work discipline, which could involve dismissal or even prison if a worker left a job without prior permission.

Fig. 9 *'Give to the heavy industry', 1927*

Fig. 10 *Propaganda poster by Vladimir Liushin: 'The organisation of communist youth is the shock brigade of the Five Year Plan'*

Fig. 11 *Propaganda poster by Adolf Strakov: 'Women, now you are free! Help us build Socialism', 1926*

■ **Cross-reference**

For more on life on collective or State farms, see Chapter 6.

In the mid-1930s, workers carried a labour book that recorded their background, their labour history and any breaking of the rules.

Therefore attitudes of workers towards the regime may well have been variable, although it is difficult to judge the extent to which ordinary workers were influenced by the regime's extensive propaganda. They were certainly not always cowed by the regime. Surviving secret police reports from the Smolensk region give extensive details of the grumblings of industrial workers and their indifference to the party leadership. When the management tried to increase work norms, workers in some factories went on strike. When 'socialist competition' was introduced, there were frequent statements such as 'competition is being carried out so that they can wring the sweat out of the workers' and 'socialist competition is bondage for the workers and prosperity for the administration'. Unskilled workers were the least content, although, as the 1930s wore on, it often became more dangerous to speak out. According to the historian Merle Fainsod (*Smolensk Under Soviet Rule*, 1989), detailed archives reveal 'a mass of unskilled and semi-skilled workers as indifferent to party appeals and smouldering with a dull resentment which they dared not or could not publically express'.

Women

Women were vital to the success of the plans. Soviet industry was very labour intensive, and about 10 million women joined the workforce during the 1930s. Their perceptions of their lives were probably as varied as their male colleagues, although women suffered additional burdens: they were usually less well paid and they received fewer training opportunities. And many had home responsibilities as well. Stalin wrote in 1937 (Source 4):

> The triumph of socialism has filled women with enthusiasm and mobilised the women of our Soviet land to become active in culture, to master machinery, to develop a knowledge of science and to be active in the struggle for high labour productivity.

4 *Quoted in D. Evans, **Stalin's Russia**, 2005*

The final claim was true: Soviet women in the 1930s were contributing greatly to labour productivity in both town and countryside. It is less certain that all women shared Stalin's enthusiasm for the triumph of Socialism, since, as well as their contribution to labour productivity in the fields and factories, the majority were also still expected to shoulder the bulk of domestic labour and childcare, just as in former times.

Convict labour

The convict empire grew greatly in the 1930s. Criminals with longer sentences were usually sent to camps, as well as 'political prisoners'. Given the hard conditions, they were not likely to be enthusiastic about the industrialisation programme, and many

Fig. 12 *Women help with threshing on a Russian collective farm*

died whilst working in the camps or on great projects such as the building of the Baltic–White Sea Canal.

Cross-reference

For details of the growth of the convict empire, see pages 106–8.

Learning outcomes

Through your study of this section you should have a good understanding of why the communist regime, and particularly Stalin, changed the NEP and introduced a policy of rapid industrialisation in the USSR at the end of the 1920s.

You should be able to explain how the various Five Year Plans operated and what their priorities were. You should be able to analyse and evaluate the results of the plans, both for the USSR as a whole and in terms of their impact on the Soviet people. You should also have some understanding of how historians have interpreted the results of the plans.

When you have read the other chapters in this book, you should also have an understanding of how industrialisation tried to correct what were seen as the faults of the NEP, and how the Five Year Plans related to other developments such as the collectivisation of agriculture and the terror of the 1930s.

AQA Examination-style questions

(a) Explain why Five Year Plans were introduced at the end of the 1920s. *(12 marks)*

AQA Examiner's tip In answering part a), it is necessary to first establish what the main aims of the plan were, covering both political and economic motives. For example, they were designed to strengthen the economy but also to lead Russia on the path towards Socialism and away from private enterprise.

(b) "The Five Year Plans were successful in strengthening the Soviet economy before 1941." Explain why you agree or disagree with this view. *(24 marks)*

AQA Examiner's tip Having answered part a), it is then possible in part b) to begin evaluating the plans' success. For example, if the main aim was to develop large-scale heavy industry, to a large extent this was achieved. If a main aim was to produce good quality goods, the level of success was much more variable. What does strengthening the economy mean? Does it include defence? Does it take the working population into account? All these and other issues might be considered.

However, as always with an essay-type question, it is important to pace yourself in the answer, keep the answer relevant, ensure that you are not telling a story but rather analysing the evidence and, finally, ensure that you make a balanced and well-supported judgement. That way you should earn high marks.

5 The political and economic motives for collectivisation

In this chapter you will learn about:

- the structure and progress of agriculture in NEP Russia
- why the USSR changed the structure of farming from 1928 onwards
- the place of agriculture in Stalin's 'economic revolution'.

Fig. 1 *Propaganda poster by Nicolai Kotcherguin: 'On the ruins of Capitalism, let us walk towards fraternity: farmers and workers are walking towards the peoples from all over the world'*

Question: What are the four reasons for the failure of Soviet agriculture?

Answer: Spring, summer, autumn and winter.

1 *A Soviet joke from the 1930s*

Agriculture before 1917

The USSR in 1928 was still an agriculturally-based society. This does not mean that farming was particularly productive. It certainly was not by western European or North American standards. What it did mean was that the majority of the population still made its living from the land. Although industrial development had taken place since the 1880s in particular, large-scale industry contributed relatively little to overall economic output.

This had always been so in the Russian Empire. Before 1861, land had been worked by **serfs**.

Serfdom was increasingly regarded as immoral (certainly by the standards of more 'advanced' societies), inefficient, an obstacle to necessary modernisation, and a potential source of major unrest or rebellion by the serfs themselves.

Therefore, Tsar Alexander II had freed the serfs in 1861. At the time, this seemed to be a radical step, and was unwelcome to landowners, who saw their source of cheap labour disappear. However, the freeing of the serfs did not fulfil its major objectives:

- The newly-freed peasants were left with heavy debts – 'redemption payments' – which they owed to the State as the price of being given land to farm.
- Agriculture did not become more efficient. There were several reasons for this, such as general poverty and lack of equipment, but a major reason was that landholdings were regularly redistributed by the village community (*mir*), so peasants without long-term security had little incentive or means to improve productivity.
- Although there were some fertile agricultural areas in Russia, much of the land was of poor quality and suffered extremes of climate. As in all Russian enterprises, poor communications hindered improvement.
- A steady rise in population and shortage of land depressed farming even more. There were several famines before 1900, and growing discontent among many peasants.

The condition of the peasantry and agriculture did not improve significantly before 1914. Redemption payments were abolished and, in the last years of peace, peasants were given the opportunity to break away from the village commune and consolidate their own holdings. But relatively few peasants took advantage of this. During the First World War, peasants suffered from the disruption and defeatism that affected all areas of Russian society.

Soviet agriculture, 1917–28

Relations between the new Soviet government and the peasantry were difficult. Lenin allowed the peasants to take over the land, which they were seizing for themeselves anyway. However, during the Civil War (1918–21), the policy of War Communism meant that the Communists seized crops from the peasants in order to feed the Red Army and workers in the towns. Many peasants rebelled in protest, many were killed and many starved.

Under the NEP, introduced in 1921, relations improved. Peasants had to pay taxes, but they could sell their crops on the open market. Some peasants, known as **kulaks**, did well, expanding their landholdings and sometimes employing other peasants. Relations between peasants and the communist regime at this stage were reasonably smooth, mainly

■ Cross-reference

For more information on the Civil War see pages 2–5. For more information on War Communism, see the Glossary.

■ Key chronology

Collectivisation

1917	Peasants seize landed estates for themselves.
	Private landownership is legalised by Lenin's communist government.
1918	Under War Communism, peasants have their crops seized from them (requisitioned) by the government.
1921	The NEP makes peasants pay a tax in kind, later in cash. Peasants are allowed to sell any surplus on the free market.
1927	Shortage of grain as peasants sow less, following a fall in grain prices.
1928	Forced seizure of grain from peasants: the 'Urals-Siberian method'.
1929	Collectivisation under way.
1930	Decree on liquidation of kulak farms.
	Temporary halt to collectivisation: Stalin issues 'Dizzy with Success' speech.
	Peasants allowed their own private plots.
1931–3	Collectivisation in full swing again.
1931–2	Extensive famine.
1932	Internal passports are issued in cities but not in countryside, restricting movement.
1934 onwards	Gradual recovery of agriculture.
1935	Peasants are allowed to sell surplus produce from private plots in collective farm markets.

because the Communist Party was town based, and so rural areas suffered little sustained interference from the authorities.

■ Soviet agriculture in 1928

The relationship between the communist regime and the countryside became more tense in 1928 for several reasons:

■ Many Communists felt it was wrong that peasants owned their own land. Private land ownership went against the communist ideal of collective ownership.

■ More food needed to be grown to support industrial progress. Workers in new industrial towns would have to be fed. The amount of grain being collected by the government was actually falling by 1928. This was because agriculture had been recovering more rapidly than industry since 1921. Consequently, peasants were getting lower prices for their food, so grew less. There were not enough goods on which peasants could spend any of their profits.

■ Agriculture was still inefficient and small scale. The regime believed that production could be increased significantly if farms were grouped together into much larger units, and machinery like tractors could be used. Fewer farm workers would be needed, and therefore labour could be transferred from the countryside to the factories in the planned new industrial towns.

■ There was a strong ideological argument going on inside the Communist Party. The right wing, associated with Bukharin, believed that the peasants should be encouraged to 'get rich' under the NEP. The resulting prosperity (meaning more tax revenue) would pay for the industrialisation that was the aim of all Communists. However, the left wing, which by now included Stalin, thought this process would be too slow and dangerous. They wanted rapid collectivisation to force the peasantry into line with their plans for industrialisation.

The situation came to a head when there was a shortage of grain in 1927–8. The government resorted to the old War Communism methods (1918–21) by sending soldiers into the countryside to forcibly take grain from the peasants. This was known as the Urals-Siberian method, named after the area where this practice was started. Peasants had not traditionally been supporters of the Communists. Stalin was no longer prepared to leave them in a position where they could blackmail the regime.

> Can the kulak be allowed to join the collective farm? Of course not! He is the accursed enemy of collectivisation.

 2   *Stalin in 1929, quoted in R. Sakwa, **The Rise and Fall of the Soviet Union**, 1999*

Stalin's attitude

As indicated above, Stalin was not happy with the existing situation by 1928. He had defeated his opponents on the left, such as Trotsky, and was about to take on Bukharin and the right. Within a year, Stalin was to effectively become the dictator of the USSR. He distrusted the peasants and was certainly not going to allow them to stand in the way of industrial progress. He saw the peasants, especially the kulaks, as class enemies who must be eliminated. Stalin was determined to wipe out any traces of Capitalism in the countryside. The fact that by following such a ruthless policy Stalin would also be removing his last political rivals such as Bukharin, and cementing his own position as leader within the party and the USSR as a whole, was an added attraction for him. Therefore political, economic, ideological and personal motives were all bound up in Stalin's decision to collectivise agriculture.

> The First Commandment is: the collective farm must make fixed deliveries of crops to the state no matter what the problems may be.

3 *From a declaration by Stalin*

> The peasants are holding their grain back, because they do not want to exchange it for money. There is a common opinion in the countryside that our money is not safe, and the opposition strengthen this belief, whispering in the peasant's ear, 'Don't take money, it's worthless.' The peasant, who is at an even lower cultural level than the city dweller, listens and becomes suspicious. The peasant supports our system, but indirectly becomes our enemy when, lacking in revolutionary consciousness and left to the propaganda of our enemies, he openly sabotages our economic programme by holding back his grain stocks.

4 *From secret Politburo discussions in January 1928*

> The effect of our huge grain deficit will be that our towns and industrial centres, as well as our Red Army, will be in grave difficulties. They will be poorly supplied and threatened with hunger. Obviously we cannot allow that. I have made a tour of Siberia and have seen for myself that there you have had a bumper harvest. Yet the plan for grain deliveries is not being met, although the kulak farms are crammed with grain. The kulaks are unwilling to deliver grain, they are waiting for prices to rise. There is no guarantee that the kulaks will not again sabotage the grain deliveries next year. It can be said with certainty that so long as there are kulaks, so long will there be sabotage of grain deliveries.

5 *Stalin, from a speech made whilst visiting Siberia, January 1928*

> Agriculture is developing slowly, comrades. The small-peasant economy does not lend itself readily to improvement. We have about 25 million individual peasant farms. It is the most insecure, the most primitive, the most undeveloped form of economic organisation. We need large farms to be run like grain factories, organised on a modern scientific basis.

6 *Stalin, April 1928*

Activity

Source analysis

Read Sources 4, 5 and 6.

1 Outline the main reasons why Stalin and his supporters were unhappy with Soviet agriculture under the NEP.

2 State any reasons why you think that these sources may be reliable or unreliable evidence for deciding why Stalin decided on collectivisation of agriculture.

Activity

Source analysis

Study Figure 2. What is the message of this cartoon, and why is it propaganda?

Fig. 2 *A Soviet cartoon from the 1920s satirising superstitious and simple peasants, manipulated by the Church. (Courtesy of John Laver)*

Collectivisation and the war against the peasantry between 1928 and the early 1930s

The process of collectivisation

Initially, in late-1928, the call went out for peasants to collectivise voluntarily. Collectivisation did not figure significantly in Stalin's First Five Year Plan. At that time, only 1.2 per cent of cultivated land was collectivised, with a further 1.5 per cent cultivated in State farms.

However, because the regime was worried about grain supplies, and relatively few peasants responded to the call to join collectives voluntarily, forcible collectivisation began in 1929. There were several stages:

- In 1929, the government issued new procurement (delivery) quotas, with punishments for peasants who did not keep up with deliveries.

- During 1929, the government launched a strong propaganda campaign against kulaks, trying to create a rift within the peasant class between poor and better-off farmers.

- By the end of 1929, the government had begun a programme of all-out, forced collectivisation. Stalin declared that kulaks must be 'liquidated as a class' and they were not permitted to join collectives.

- Peasants were driven into collectives by local Communists, backed up by the security police (OGPU) and Red Army where necessary.

- Strong opposition from the peasantry led Stalin to a temporary climbdown in March 1930. He declared in an article called 'Dizzy with Success' that local officials were too rigorous and confrontational in carrying out collectivisation. Many peasants were allowed to leave collectives and had their livestock returned to them, provided they were not kulaks.

Stalin's climbdown was only a temporary tactic. Once the peasants had sown the spring crop, the process of collectivisation speeded up again, with peasants forced or persuaded to sign up to collectives. Soviet sources claimed that by 1932, 62 per cent of peasant households had been collectivised, and 93 per cent by 1937.

Fig. 3 *Peasants holding a placard that reads: 'We, as kolkhozniks (collective farmers), will eradicate the kulaks, following the total collectivisation principle'*

Opposition to collectivisation

On the left a sickle

On the right a hammer

That's our Soviet emblem.

So whether you reap the corn

Or strike the anvil

Either way

You get **** all

7

A Soviet joke from the 1930s

There was widespread and violent opposition to the process of collectivisation, amounting to civil war in the countryside. Although some, mainly poorer peasants, joined collectives voluntarily, most peasants did not. Peasants from more fertile agricultural areas like the Ukraine were particularly hostile. Many peasants burned their farms and crops and killed their livestock rather than hand them over. The armed forces brutally dealt with unrest by bombing villages and deporting millions of peasants to remote areas such as Siberia, often to labour camps. Others went to the new industrial towns. Any peasant who resisted was classified as a kulak and a class enemy. Probably over 10 million peasants died as the result of resistance or the effects of deportation. By 1939, about 19 million peasants had migrated to towns: in effect, for every three peasants who joined a collective, one left the countryside to become an urban or industrial wage earner.

Those who refuse to join collectives are called kulaks, dispossessed of all they own and are sent to the north with their families. Those peasants who do enter the collectives first slaughter their cattle. It seems just as well to gorge themselves with meat for once in their lives and secretly sell the leather, as to give their cattle to the state. In 1932 the state declares socialist property sacred. Its theft is punished by death.

| 8 | *From V. Serge, **From Lenin to Stalin**, 1973* |

80 peasants in this hole-in-the-ground came to the public prosecutor to complain that they had been forced by violence to join the collective. In this area presidents of collective farms have been assassinated. For a long time we have seen neither meat nor fish. The peasants have replied to forced collectivisation by selling their possessions, sabotaging the work and rebelling.

| 9 | *From letters written in the countryside in 1930* |

Many peasants with their traditional petty-owner mentality were psychologically unprepared to become members of collective farms, and even when they did join, continued to waver for a time. Hesitation and doubt increased under the impact of the kulaks' unceasing agitation, for example urging peasants to slaughter their farm animals, which would allegedly be taken from them. Kulak agitation was often effective. As a result, the livestock population in the USSR dropped by 25 per cent. The USSR's enemies portray the kulaks as the true spokesmen for the entire peasantry, and regret the fact that the kulaks departed from the arena of history. These enemies exaggerate the shortcomings and mistakes committed during collectivisation, and ignore the fact that the Party put right these mistakes. They prefer to ignore the main thing – the tremendous importance that collectivisation has had for the progress of the countryside and of the entire nation towards socialism.

| 10 | *From a Soviet history book published in 1981* |

Activity

Source analysis

Study Sources 8, 9 and 10.

1 Outline the main difficulties caused by the process of collectivisation.

2 Identify elements of propaganda in these sources. Does this affect the value of these sources as evidence about collectivisation?

What was a collective farm?

Roosevelt, Churchill and Stalin went to inspect a collective farm. They had to cross over a bridge, but there was a cow standing on it, in the way.

Churchill got out of the car and approached the cow to get it out of the way.

'Moo-o-o' went the cow and lowered her horns at Churchill. Churchill retreated.

Then Roosevelt approached.

'Moo-o-o' went the cow, lowering its horns. Roosevelt backed off.

Stalin came up and whispered something to the cow. The cow took off in fright.

'What did you say to her, Joseph?' asked Churchill and Roosevelt.

'I told her that if she did not get out of the way I would put her in a collective farm.'

11
A post-war Soviet joke

Fig. 4 *Meeting of kolkhoz workers at harvesting. The poster reads: 'Farm workers say "Go to the collectives"', 1929*

Collective farms are often portrayed as huge units. In reality, few very large farms survived the early days of collectivisation. Most collectives were essentially made up of the old village, and peasants lived in the same houses as before. What changed was the management and what was done with the produce.

The typical features of a collective farm (*kolkhoz*) are described below:

- There were about 240,000 collective farms by 1940.

- The **average** collective contained 76 families, and had 60 cattle, 94 sheep and goats, and 26 pigs.

- From 1930, the old village council or *mir* was replaced by an appointed chairman, who was a Communist Party member who volunteered or was sent from a town. Therefore rural areas were put under communist control for the first time.

- The farm had to deliver a set amount of produce to the State. Quotas were high: up to 40 per cent of crops. A low purchase price was set by the government.

- Any profit left over was shared out among the collective members according to their work contribution.

- Machine Tractor Stations (MTS) were set up to hire tractors to collective farms. However, mechanisation never became widespread. By 1940, there was one MTS for every 40 collective farms.

■ Some collectives did receive social benefits, such as a school or clinic – but at the expense of peasants losing any individual freedom.

■ A relatively small number of farms were run as State farms (*sovkhoz*) rather than collectives: in other words, the people who worked these farms were employed and paid a wage directly by the State. They were classified as 'workers' rather than 'peasants'.

Summary questions

1 How successful was Soviet agriculture under the NEP?

2 Explain why Stalin carried out a programme of collectivisation in the 1930s.

3 Explain why Stalin acted ruthlessly towards the peasants in the 1930s.

6 The impact of collectivisation on the USSR to 1941

In this chapter you will learn about:

- how collectivisation affected the peasantry

- how collectivisation affected agriculture

- how collectivisation affected the economy as a whole

- the political consequences of collectivisation.

A Party commissar was visiting a collective farm to check up on the season's crops.

'How are the potatoes?' he asked.

'There are so many potatoes,' a farmer replied, 'that if we laid them end to end they would touch the feet of God.'

'How can that be?' exclaimed the commissar. 'There is no God.'

'Well, there are no potatoes either.'

1   *A Soviet joke from the 1930s*

Fig. 1 *Propaganda poster by Vasily Yefanov: 'Not a single parcel of land without farming', 1930*

Collectivisation was a major part of Stalin's second revolution, whereby he transformed the USSR's economy and society in his bid to create his version of Socialism. The impact on the Soviet countryside was dramatic, and affected Soviet agriculture down to the break-up of the USSR in 1991. There were economic, political and social repercussions.

The various impacts of collectivisation

Economic impact

The economic impact of collectivisation was enormous:

- During the disruption of collectivisation and the period of peasant opposition, agricultural production fell dramatically (sometimes even to 1913 levels), and did not recover until well into the late-1930s.

- There was widespread famine in 1932–3, especially in the Ukraine, Kazakhstan and the Caucasus. Millions of peasants died. Many of the most skilled and successful farmers disappeared for good.

- The State secured the grain it wanted. It was able to supply the towns with food, and also export grain to pay for imports of technology. Collectivisation enabled Stalin's industrialisation programme to continue throughout the 1930s.

- Agriculture remained the poor relation of the Soviet economy. Farming remained inefficient, often unproductive and with poor levels of mechanisation. Peasants lacked the incentive to work hard. Many worked much harder on the small private plots that Stalin allowed them as a concession during collectivisation.

- From 1932, collectives were allowed to sell grain left over from State procurements in a collective farm market – the only free markets allowed in the USSR. From 1935, peasants could also sell produce from their private plots in these markets. Eventually, private plots produced about one-third of all marketed food in the USSR, although they made up only about 4 per cent of cultivated land.

Political impact

The political impact of collectivisation was equally important for Stalin:

- For the first time, the Soviet regime had extended its political control over the countryside, mainly through party management of the collectives. Never again would peasants be able to resist the regime nor hold it to ransom.

- It reinforced Stalin's control within the USSR and over the Communist Party. Those on the right who opposed collectivisation, such as Bukharin and Rykov, lost power and influence.

- It moved the USSR further along the road towards Stalin's version of Socialism. Class differences in the countryside were abolished. Apart from the existence of small private plots, any remains of Capitalism, based on private enterprise, had been destroyed.

Social impact

The social impact of collectivisation is less easy to pin down than the economic impact, but was still significant:

- Millions of peasants died or had their lives totally disrupted.

- Although internal passports were introduced in 1932, restricting movement, millions of younger people left the countryside for the towns, leaving a serious population imbalance in rural areas.

Activity

Thinking point

Using Figures 1 and 2, what information can be obtained about the overall aims of collectivisation?

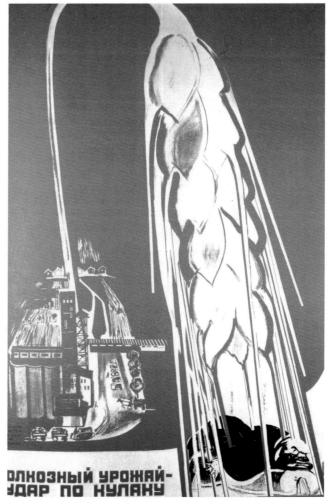

Fig. 2 *Propaganda poster by Josif Gromitsky: 'The aim of the production of collective farms is to crush Capitalism', 1931*

Many peasants felt a sense of betrayal and hostility towards the regime, regarding their condition as a 'new serfdom'. As a result, some welcomed the German invasion of 1941, hoping for liberation from the collectives, although this may also have been partly a natural reaction by people desperate to accommodate a dangerous enemy.

Although collectivisation brought some benefits to the countryside, such as education, rural Russia was regarded as the poor relation of the new urban USSR. Collectivisation was part of the process by which the USSR changed from being an agricultural nation to an industrial nation. In the process, agriculture was clearly sacrificed to the needs of industry as well as to Soviet ideology.

Question: What does it mean when there is food in the town but no food in the countryside?

Answer: A Left, Trotskyist deviation.

Question: What does it mean when there is food in the countryside but no food in the town?

Answer: A Right, Bukharinite deviation.

Question: What does it mean when there is no food in the countryside and no food in the town?

Answer: The correct application of the Party general line.

Question: And what does it mean when there is food both in the countryside and in the town?

Answer: The horrors of capitalism.

2 *A Communist Party joke from 1932*

Activity

Talking point

As a class, debate the following: 'Did the advantages of collectivisation outweigh the disadvantages?'

Fig. 3 *The fight for the harvest: sorting seeds in a collective farm, 1933*

Activity

Thinking point

1. Read the following statements. Which do you agree with and which do you disagree with?

   - Agriculture was the weakest sector of the Russian/Soviet economy before 1928.
   - Collectivisation considerably improved Soviet agriculture.
   - Kulaks were a threat to social stability in the USSR.
   - Collectivisation was a well-planned process.
   - Stalin's motives for collectivisation were political rather than economic.
   - Most peasants welcomed collectivisation.
   - Peasants had gained little from the NEP.
   - Collectivisation benefited Soviet industry.
   - Industrialisation could not have taken place without collectivisation.
   - Peasants were better off after collectivisation than before.
   - The Communist Party gained most from collectivisation.
   - Bukharin's ideas for agriculture were impractical.
   - Collectivisation would not have taken place without Stalin.
   - The Communist Party was stronger in urban areas than rural ones.
   - Collectivisation sacrificed human wellbeing to the political needs of the State.

2. Identify which of the above statements are fact, and which are opinion. Are any of them both?

Socialist Russia meant an industrial Russia. Agriculture did not receive from Stalin the same attention as industry. The process of collectivisation was a human tragedy on a gigantic scale, involving millions of deaths and the disruption of an equal number of lives. Stalin admitted to Churchill during the Second World War that the policy of carrying through collectivisation had caused him more stress than the war against Germany. Nevertheless, Stalin expressed no real regret, and would have regarded collectivisation as a political success, since it was part of his transformation of the NEP into Socialist Russia, and part of the consolidation of his own power inside the USSR.

Interpretations of collectivisation

There have been various interpretations of collectivisation, particularly the reasons for it.

One argument is that Stalin had clear economic and political motives, and so planned and carried out the process, once he was in power.

Stalin was aware of the **economic** arguments about the best way forward for Soviet agriculture (relating to opportunities for mechanisation, greater productivity, etc.) It was never likely that most peasants would willingly give up their land, and therefore Stalin was prepared to use force to make the change from the NEP.

Additionally, Stalin had **political** aims. He wanted to increase his power over the party, having recently defeated both left and right in the struggle to consolidate power in the years following Lenin's death. He saw the movement to collectivisation not just as a means of advancing the USSR towards Socialism, but as a means of trouncing his rivals, particularly

Bukharin and his followers, who were opposed to rapid, forced collectivisation. One historian wrote (Source 3):

> The break with NEP had little to do with the wishes of the party rank and file or the wishes of any other social group. It was instead a preemptive strike of the central party-state apparatus… It was as much a strike at the party, which was, in effect, an autonomous local elite tied to the peasantry, as it was a blow against entrepreneurial peasantry. It was a policy designed to strengthen the centre's control over the provinces and their provincial party cliques… It was a new war on society to preserve the dictatorship. It was a matter of constructing a centralised state, to be represented as 'constructing socialism'.

3   *V. Brovkin,* **Russia After Lenin***, 1998*

In short, it was part of the process that had begun soon after the 1917 Revolution when Lenin and his colleagues not only imposed a dictatorship over Russia, but sought to centralise power in themselves, beginning with reducing the power of local Soviets that allowed too much leeway to provincial party members.

Another interpretation is that Stalin did not plan an agricultural revolution but got caught up in a process that was not controlled by any one person. Differences in the development rates of industry and agriculture showed that the NEP was only a partial success. In particular, there was a shortage of grain on the market, leading to the Procurement Crisis. Therefore the party had to do something, and requisitioning led on to dekulakisation and collectivisation, but this was not carefully planned in advance. Even in 1929, nobody knew what collectivised agriculture would look like in practice. Stalin was prepared to use force, since he was used to doing that, but this does not mean that he knew exactly where he was going.

Fig. 4 *Farmers on their way to work on the collective farm*

Fig. 5 *A 1920s cartoon about the peasantry: 'Before: one with the plough, seven with a spoon. Now: He who does not work shall not eat.' (Courtesy of John Laver)*

Historians such as Arch Getty believe that the idea of Stalin initiating all policies and riding roughshod over everyone else is exaggerated. For example, there is plenty of evidence to suggest widespread support in the USSR for the campaign against kulaks, with many industrial and urban workers joining in demonstrations and implementation of the policy from 1929.

There is another interpretation which combines those outlined above. Collectivisation had always been a long-term party objective (although according to Lenin, to be achieved 'voluntarily'). But in the later 1920s, those on the left felt that an attack on kulaks as representatives of Capitalism was necessary to discredit the ideas of the right, which seemed to be encouraging capitalist development. This fitted in with a growing awareness of the need for reliable and cheap food supplies to support industry and national defence requirements. It also fitted in with Stalin's own political agenda and offered an apparently quick solution to problems. Stalin's actions were usually driven by a combination of what he viewed as the country's needs and his own desire for power. Stalin was driven by results, and was fond of discrediting theoretical analysis with the argument that '"science" has a lot to learn from practice'.

Activity

Source analysis

Consider the interpretations and the cartoon (Figure 5) above.

1. What elements of propaganda can you identify in the cartoon?

2. Is it effective as propaganda?

3. Does the cartoon give a convincing picture of the importance of the peasant in Stalin's scheme of things?

4. Which of the interpretations of Stalin's treatment of agriculture do you find most convincing, and why?

Activity

Revision exercise

Copy and complete the following table in order to test your own knowledge of the topic of collectivisation 1928–41.

Features of topic	Details	Notes
Main features of collectivisation	Aims	
	Methods	
	Results	
	Justification	
Key dates		
Key people involved		
Key terms		
Key issues	Economic	
	Political	
	Social	
	Other	
Key interpretations		
Other aspects		

Learning outcomes

Through your study of this section you should be familiar with the various reasons why Soviet agriculture went through a period of dramatic and turbulent change in the years from 1928 onwards. You should be able to explain why the various motives were linked, and show understanding of the turbulent nature of the actual process of collectivisation. You should understand the consequences of the process – political, social and economic – and have some awareness of why this is still a controversial topic, even beyond 1941, since collectivisation had a long-term as well as short-term impact.

When you have studied other chapters in this book you will also have some understanding of the link between agriculture and other aspects of Soviet history during this period, such as industrialisation and Stalin's terror.

AQA Examination-style questions

Read Sources A, B and C below and answer the questions that follow.

Developments from the mid-1930s may have improved the peasants' attitude towards the state. Living standards were rising slowly, although higher demands for food deliveries in 1939–41 stirred up some dissatisfaction. The state, having realised that it could not control the peasants' daily lives, began to regularise its demands on the farmers. In turn, the farmers learned to manoeuvre within the system to escape its harshest effects. By the later 1930s, collective farmers had gained more say over who their chairpersons would be. In 1937 collective farmers wrote to Stalin and other officials with various complaints. Although improvements hardly produced a comfortable life or overrode memories of collectivisation, they may have made many farmers feel that still better times were on the way. Young collective farmers were more positively disposed towards Stalin's regime than older ones.

A
*Adapted from R. Thurston, **Life and Terror in Stalin's Russia 1934–1941**, Yale University Press, 1996*

The restructuring of the agrarian economy could have been accomplished entirely without recourse to the terror and the tragedy that exceeded the repressions of 1937–38. The use of force was criminal. The successful 'liquidation of the kulaks' inflated Stalin's confidence in himself as a dictator. Stalin's forced 'agrarian revolution' condemned Soviet agriculture to decades of stagnation. The bloody revolution costing millions of lives brought the country no relief. Fear and apathy descended on the village. The first victim of Stalinism was the peasant. By taking the unprecedented decision to use force against his own people, Stalin cut the veins of a vast social group that had greatly benefited from the revolution and could have made good use of that benefit.

B
The overall effect of collectivisation described by the Russian historian Dmitri Volkogonov in 1988

I was convinced that we were warriors on an invisible front, fighting against kulak sabotage for the grain which was needed by the country, but also for the souls of these peasants who succumbed to enemy agitation, who did not understand the great truth of communism. I took part in plundering raids, taking food and livestock and also valuables. The women howled hysterically. I heard the children echoing them with screams. And I persuaded myself not to give in to pity. We were carrying out our revolutionary duty and historical necessity. It was necessary to clench your teeth, clench your heart and carry out everything the party and the Soviet power ordered.

C
*Adapted from L. Kopolev, '**The Education of a True Believer**', 1981*

(a) Explain how far the views in Source B
     differ from those in Source A in relation
     to the impact of collectivisation.   *(12 marks)*

AQA
Examiner's tip
Part a) requires you to do two different things. Firstly, read both Sources A and B carefully, and comment on any similarities and differences between them. Comment on both content and tone. Clearly the overall tone is different: basically the author of Source A suggests that, although there were problems, perhaps the worst was over by the mid-1930s: some farmers at least were feeling more positive about their situation, they were confident about complaining, and were becoming slightly better off. In contrast, Source B is extremely critical of the whole process, asserting that it was unnecessary, 'criminal', on a huge scale, and damaged the USSR for generations. Neither source gives much specific evidence. Your answer will probably be better if you make the source comparison explicit throughout the answer, rather than simply dealing with each source in turn.

You should then consider why there might be a difference in the sources. You are given some information in the attributions of the sources: one author is Russian, the other American. The Russian was writing soon after the introduction of *glasnost* or 'openness' in the USSR, when historians were just beginning to write more openly about their past. Source A was written slightly later. Source A is about the later 1930s; Source B is covering the earlier phase of collectivisation. Do these facts influence the interpretations?

(b) Use Sources A, B and C and your own knowledge.
How successful was collectivisation in
transforming Soviet agriculture by 1941?   *(24 marks)*

Part b) is testing your knowledge of the topic and your ability to write a relevant, structured answer in the form of a short essay. You may find it helpful to construct a short plan to marshal your thoughts. Have a clear line of argument before you start. Consider the key words such as 'successful' and 'transforming'. What does 'successful' mean in this context? Collectivisation was probably successful in realising Stalin's ambition of getting rid of kulaks and gaining firm control of the countryside, but what about the human cost? What was the impact on production and on the Soviet economy as a whole? The organisation of farming was certainly transformed to some extent, but was it for the better? Did it depend on where you were in the Soviet social structure? Do we now have a better perspective on events? It will certainly improve your answer if you can consider both the short-term and long-term consequences. Don't forget that you will need to refer to all 3 sources as evidence in your answer. For a good mark there should be a clear judgement in your answer, either clearly developed towards the end or present throughout the answer, and you should ensure that your argument is consistent.

7 The Great Terror and the purges

In this chapter you will learn about:

- the background of the purges and the impact of Kirov's assassination

- the motives for the terror

- the course of the terror and who carried it out

- different interpretations of the terror.

Activity

Thinking point

Why do you think people told such jokes when it was dangerous to do so?

Activity

Source analysis

Study Figure 1. What is the message of this cartoon?

A man on a long train ride was alone and bored. He was overjoyed when another man entered his compartment. 'I'm glad you're here,' he exclaimed. 'I was so bored before you arrived. Now I can tell you all the new jokes I've heard recently.'

'Before you begin, I ought to warn you I'm from the secret police.'

'Oh, that's all right,' the first man said. 'I'll tell the jokes very slowly, and I'll even repeat them for you.'

1 *A Soviet joke from the 1930s*

Fig. 1 *Stalin dominating the government. A cartoon published in Paris by Russians who had fled from Stalin's rule. (Courtesy of John Laver)*

Activity

Source analysis

Read Source 2. Do you think Bukharin's views were correct? If so, why should the people to whom Bukharin refers have been bitter and hostile towards Stalin?

The main reason for Stalin's decision to carry out the Terror was his realisation, based on reports reaching him, that the mood of most old Party workers was really one of bitterness and hostility towards him

2 *Bukharin, letter of an Old Bolshevik, 1938*

The Kirov murder (1934) and its effects

Background to terror

Purges and terror had been features of communist rule in the USSR since the revolution. Periodic purges usually meant the dismissal of Communist Party members for political untrustworthiness, 'errors', or 'anti-social deviant behaviour' such as alcoholism. During the 1930s, purging could mean something much more drastic, resulting in imprisonment or death. The Great Terror itself is usually dated from the aftermath of the Kirov assassination in 1934, and lasting until 1939.

Terror (or 'coercion') was born out of the ruthlessness of the Civil War period of 1918–21. In these years of struggle, Lenin had used any means to crush internal and external enemies of Bolshevik rule – the so-called 'Red Terror'. After the more relaxed period of NEP Russia (1921–8), a new clampdown on freedom coincided with Stalin's emergence as leader and the beginnings of the campaigns for collectivisation and industrialisation. Stalin's reasoning to the party on the need for force was reflected in a speech (Source 3):

Cross-reference

For more details on the terrors of the Civil War period, see pages 2–5. For information on collectivisation and industrialisation, see Chapters 3–6.

As the USSR starts on the road to Socialism, so its enemies will become more desperate in their efforts to destroy us, and we must be ever more vigilant.

3   *Taken from a speech made by Stalin in the early 1930s*

Key chronology

1927	Trotsky, Zinoviev and Kamenev are expelled from the party.
1928	Trial of 53 engineers and technicians for anti-Soviet activities – Shakhty trial.
1929	Trotsky is expelled from the USSR.
	Bukharin is sacked from Politburo.
1930	Collectivisation and coercion of kulaks.
	Trial of engineers for sabotage and treason.
1931	Trial of several former Mensheviks and SRs.
1932	Suicide of Stalin's wife Nadezhda Alliluyeva.
	Ryutin is denounced for opposing Stalin.
1933	One sixth of party members are expelled.
	Trial of British engineers for 'sabotage' (Metro-Vickers trial).
1934	Party purge.
	17th Party Congress.
	GPU is reorganised as **NKVD**.
	Assassination of Kirov.
1935	Zinoviev and Kamenev are imprisoned.
	Nine per cent of party is expelled.
1936	Show trial and execution of Zinoviev and Kamenev.
	Yezhov replaces Yagoda as security chief.
	Beginning of the Great Purge.
	Purge of police and security services.
1937	Show trial of 'Trotskyists', including Radek.
	Ordzhonikidze commits suicide.
	Tukachevsky is tried and executed.
	Purge of Red Army.
1938	Bukharin, Rykov, Yagoda and 'Rightists' are tried and executed.
	Beria succeeds Yezhov as security chief.
1939	Relaxation of the terror announced by Stalin.
1940	Assassination of Trotsky in Mexico.

Key term

NKVD: Stalin's secret police. The GPU had been replaced by the OGPU in 1923 and the NKVD in 1934. Genrikh Yagoda was the Head of the NKVD from 1934 until his replacement in 1936 by Nikolai Yezhov, who was replaced himself in 1938 by Lavrenti Beria. Both Yagoda and Yezhov were themselves victims of Stalin. Beria survived Stalin but was arrested almost immediately after his death.

Even before the watershed of the Kirov assassination, there were signs of an increasingly hard line approach by the regime.

■ **The Shakhty trial** (1928). One of a series of trials of industrial specialists from middle-class or foreign backgrounds. They were accused of sabotage, spying or anti-Socialism. Some of the victims were shot.

■ **Ryutin**. In 1932, the former Central Committee member Mikhail Ryutin published a pamphlet highly critical of Stalin's leadership and methods. Stalin could only get him imprisoned, but Ryutin was eventually executed in 1937.

■ In 1933, six **British engineers** were tried for industrial espionage.

Even before the Kirov affair, Stalin's ruthlessness had already been in evidence. In 1930, Mikhail Ryutin, a former Central Committee member and party secretary for Moscow, had been expelled from the party for anti-Stalinist views. In 1932, he published a document describing Stalin as 'the evil genius of the Russian Revolution', and 'motivated by personal desire for power and revenge'. Stalin was 'the most evil enemy of the party and the proletarian dictatorship'. He should be removed from power and extreme policies such as collectivisation should be reversed. Ryutin was imprisoned in a labour camp until the all-powerful Stalin had him executed in 1937. He was given a 40-minute trial and then immediately executed. Ryutin's two sons were also executed, and one of his daughters-in-law went insane. Stalin was aware that there were other prominent Communists who had serious doubts about his leadership and policies, and was probably fearful that another, more popular, Communist might act as a focus for discontent and challenge his position. Hence the controversy over Stalin's behaviour in the subsequent Kirov affair.

The Kirov assassination

Sergei Kirov is often portrayed as one of the most popular Communist leaders. Born in 1886, and an orphan from an early age, he organised strikes during the 1905 Revolution. Kirov fought for the Red Army in the Civil War and soon joined the Central Committee. He was made head of the Leningrad Party organisation in 1926. Kirov later became a member of the Politburo and a close companion of Stalin, often holidaying with him. He was regarded by many as Stalin's eventual successor – a dangerous reputation to have in itself! Kirov has sometimes been regarded as one of the more liberal Communists, an outstanding orator, popular and accessible to ordinary people. But others regarded him as corrupt and vicious, a hardliner who supported Stalin on most issues and had few doubts about the party's direction.

Fig. 2 *Sergei Kirov, Bolshevik revolutionary leader and Soviet politician, who was assassinated in Leningrad on 1 December, 1934*

For example, at the 17th Party Congress he commented on the recently built Baltic–White Sea Canal:

> to build such a canal, in such a short time and in such a place is a really heroic labour, and we must give credit to our Chekists who supervised the work and literally performed miracles.

He did not mention that the real work had been done by thousands of slave labourers.

Nevertheless, Kirov was prepared to argue with Stalin over some policies. In 1932, Kirov opposed Stalin's attempt to have Ryutin executed. In 1933, Stalin appointed the rising star Kirov as a party secretary in Moscow, in order to remove him from his power base in Leningrad. However, Kirov upset Stalin further by requesting to stay in Leningrad, and stood against Stalin for the post of General Secretary when it came up for election at the 1934 17th Party Congress. Kirov was the only significant figure to pose any sort of challenge to Stalin. Others at the Congress fell over themselves in their haste to praise Stalin, even for the way he had defeated them a few years before. Bukharin declared:

> Stalin was entirely correct when he smashed a whole series of theoretical arguments of the **Right Deviation**, which had been formulated above all by myself... It is the duty of every party member to rally round Comrade Stalin.

Kamenev and Zinoviev had been working hard to get back into Stalin's favour. Zinoviev declared at the Congress:

> We now know that the struggle which Comrade Stalin conducted was on an exclusively high theoretical level. We know that in this struggle there was not the least hint of anything personal.

Kamenev declared of himself:

> The Kamenev who from 1925 to 1933 struggled with the party and its leadership, I regard as a political corpse. I want to go forward, without dragging the old skin after me. Long live our leader and commander Comrade Stalin.

We cannot be certain what Stalin thought of these humiliating climbdowns by previous opponents, although their grovelling did not save them in the forthcoming terror. Of more immediate concern to Stalin was Kirov. On the last day of the Congress a secret ballot was held to confirm Stalin in the role of General Secretary. Stalin was told that almost a quarter of the delegates had voted against him. The organisers of the ballot were alarmed at the possible consequences. Stalin was told of the result, and most of the ballot papers were destroyed. A group of Old Bolsheviks, aware that Lenin's testament had proposed removing Stalin from power years before, tried to persuade Kirov to stand against Stalin for the role of General Secretary. Kirov refused and supposedly told Stalin. That was apparently enough for Stalin to regard Kirov as a real rival.

Soon afterwards, Kirov was assassinated outside his Leningrad headquarters. The circumstances were mysterious. Kirov's bodyguard, who witnessed the shooting, was killed on the following day in a road accident whilst travelling with KGB agents. The assassin, Nikolaev, insisted that he had acted alone, but was executed with several other alleged accomplices.

The Kirov assassination had important consequences:

■ Whether Stalin was implicated or not (Stalin's daughter maintained that the assassination was actually the work of the NKVD and one of its ruthless and ambitious leaders, Lavrenti Beria), Stalin used the event as an excuse to implement a reign of terror, first against leading party or ex-party members.

■ A law in December 1934 speeded up the process of trying suspects and removed any right of appeal. Soon afterwards, Kamenev, Zinoviev and Yagoda, the secret police chief, were arrested.

■ The assassination and its aftermath showed that nobody was safe, no matter how important they were.

■ The assassination became the signal for the regime to tighten its hold over the country and begin a reign of widespread purges, a period that became known as the Great Terror. Some historians have argued that Stalin's most extreme behaviour dates from this period: his suspicion of plots and rivals, which verged on paranoia; his vindictiveness towards those who had crossed him in the past; his determination to allow no limits to his power or his policies; and his determination to exercise strict control over both party and country.

Fig. 3 *Stalin and Kirov, 1930*

The motives for the purges and the Great Terror

A particular feature of the wave of terror that swept over the USSR was the **Show Trials** of prominent Communists. These were trials whose outcomes had already been determined, because the defendants had been persuaded or tortured into confession. Sometimes they were even persuaded that confession to 'crimes' was in the interests of the party and the revolution. The Show Trials were an opportunity for Stalin to demonstrate to his people and the outside world that the regime meant business in protecting the forward march to Socialism. Therefore the trials were highly publicised, with foreign journalists present. Stalin is supposed to have watched court proceedings from a hidden vantage point.

At the same time as the Show Trials were taking place, millions of other Soviet citizens were tried, imprisoned, deported or executed, with a major impact on the Soviet economy and society.

Key term

Show Trials: propaganda exercises in which important prisoners were tried publicly, but the verdicts had already been decided beforehand, with agreed confessions. They were used so that the regime could get maximum publicity to justify its activities.

Cross-reference

For the effects of Stalin's persecutions on the Soviet economy and society see Chapters 4 and 6.

Fig. 4 *A Soviet cartoon showing Social Democracy and Capitalism making an alliance which reads: 'War against the USSR.' (Courtesy of John Laver)*

Interpretations of motives for the terror

Various interpretations have been put forward to explain the Great Terror. The main ones are:

Fig. 5 *A 1933 Soviet cartoon called 'Karl Marx and Pygmies' (Courtesy of John Laver)*

■ it was due to Stalin's personality, which made him suspicious, vindictive, and even paranoid. He was obsessed with reinforcing his own position, eliminating possible rivals, and wreaking revenge on fellow Bolsheviks (the 'Old Guard') who had been his rivals or opponents before the 1930s.

■ terror was an integral part of the communist system, and indeed of earlier Russian regimes, albeit then on a smaller scale. The 1917 Revolution and its aftermath, the Civil War, saw the communist regime born in terror, and then maintained by terror. Stalin simply applied terror more ruthlessly and on a larger scale than Lenin had done, once he had the power to do so.

■ terror was a necessary part of the process of economic change taking place from the late-1920s. This change was often forced on unwilling groups such as kulaks. Slave labour provided by the huge labour camp complex was an important part of the drive to raise production. People were also purged because scapegoats were needed to explain away mistakes and failure to meet targets.

■ fear of the foreign enemies surrounding the USSR bred fear and suspicion, especially after Hitler came to power in Germany in 1933. Hitler was known to be violently anti-communist.

■ over-zealous party officials in the provinces sometimes acted ruthlessly and followed their own agenda, independently of Moscow. Therefore the drive to terror did not come exclusively from Stalin.

■ in 1937, Marshall Tukhachevsky, despite being a civil war hero and one of the founders of the Red Army, was tried and shot, followed by over 35,000 officers. Stalin wanted total control of the armed forces and seems to have genuinely believed that there was a military plot against him, probably involving the Germans. Some historians believe that the Germans deliberately fed these suspicions, counting on Stalin acting against his generals and thereby weakening the USSR. There had certainly been contacts between the Red Army and the Nazis under earlier treaties and Stalin was always likely to be suspicious.

■ **Activity**

Talking point

1 Study Figures 4 and 5. What message is being put across in each of these cartoons?

2 From what you already know of the 1930s USSR, how effective do you think these cartoons would have been as propaganda?

3 From your own knowledge, explain how useful these two cartoons are to a historian as explanations for the terror.

■ Cross-reference

For more on the role of other individuals in the terror see pages 94–6.

The views of some of the participants

I plead guilty to being one of the leaders of the bloc of 'Rightists' and Trotskyites, irrespective of whether I knew of or took part in any particular act.

 4   *A statement by Bukharin during his trial proceedings in 1938*

Harshness was necessary. After the Revolution we slashed Right and Left. We scored victories, but tattered remnants of enemies survived. As we were faced by the growing danger of fascist aggression in 1937, these enemies might have united. Yes, mistakes were made, but terror was necessary. The alternative was to carry internal political debates into the war of 1941.

5   *Adapted from 'Molotov Remembers', 1993*

Molotov was a close colleague of Stalin and became Foreign Minister in 1939. His wife was a later victim of the purges, although Molotov stayed loyal to his master.

The only purpose of terror is intimidation: to plunge the whole country into a state of chronic fear. The remaining inhabitants will be model citizens for the rest of their lives.

 6   *Taken from Nadezhda Mandelstam's memoirs*

The Trotskyites and Bukharinites are not a political party but a band of felonious criminals who have sold themselves to enemy intelligence services. They are the most contemptible, the most depraved of the depraved. Our whole country, from young to old, is demanding one thing: the traitors and spies who were selling our country to the enemy must be shot like dirty dogs! Our people are demanding one thing: crush the accursed reptile!

7   *Adapted from a speech by Andrei Vishinsky, chief prosecutor in the Show Trials, 1938*

Nadezhda was the wife of the poet Osip Mandelstam, arrested in 1934.

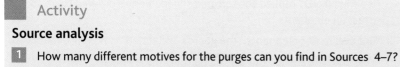

Activity

Source analysis

1 How many different motives for the purges can you find in Sources 4–7?

2 Identify which sources are pro-Stalin and anti-Stalin. Using your own knowledge, explain which sources give the most convincing explanations of the purges.

Fig. 6 *Campaign to purge the party. Meeting in Astrakhan in 1929. Members of the ruling team of the sawmill interrogated about their social origin*

Activity

Revision exercise

Use the information in this chapter to make your own timeline of what you believe to be the most important features of the terror.

Activity

Thinking point

What is the message of the jokes in Source 8?

The course of the terror and the role of Stalin and other key individuals

A man was sitting in his flat and he heard a loud knock on the door.

'Who is it?' he asked fearfully.

'It's the Angel of Death.'

'Thank God!' the man replied. 'For a moment I thought it was the secret police.'

Question: Why do Soviet doctors remove tonsils through the backside?

Answer: Because nobody dares open their mouth.

Stalin's pipe is missing. He calls the NKVD and orders them to find it. Two hours later he finds it himself in a cupboard and calls the NKVD back: 'Don't bother, I've found it.'

'Forgive us, Comrade Stalin, but we've already arrested ten people for stealing your pipe.'

'Let them go.'

'We can't, they've all confessed.'

A flock of sheep was stopped by frontier guards at the Russo-Finnish border.

'Why do you want to leave Russia?' the guards demanded.

'It's the NKVD,' replied the terrified sheep. 'Beria's ordered them to arrest all elephants.'

'But you're not elephants!' the guards exclaimed.

'Yes,' said the sheep. 'But try telling that to the NKVD!'

| 8 | *Four jokes secretly circulating in the USSR in the 1930s* |

Certain individuals and organisations played a key role in the terror. Although there has long been a historical debate about the exact extent of Stalin's role in the terror, compared to other factors at work, there can be little doubt that Stalin's role was crucial both in beginning the purges and ending them (at least temporarily: they resumed again both during and after the Second World War).

Stalin's role in the terror

Background

Stalin was no stranger to violence. From his earliest Bolshevik days he had been a man of action and an organiser rather than a theoretician, and had risen through the party ranks precisely because he had a reputation for getting things done. He had shown no qualms about manoeuvring himself to power during the 1920s, and isolating and driving his rivals out of the party. Nevertheless, there was little to anticipate the scale of the terror in the 1930s, other than Stalin's ruthless persecution of the peasantry once collectivisation had begun. A key moment that led to the institutionalisation of the terror appears to have been the suicide of Stalin's wife, Nadezhda Alliluyeva, in 1932. She was highly strung, had a stormy relationship with Stalin and was upset at his treatment of the peasantry. Following one of her stormy arguments with Stalin, she shot

Did you know?

In his early days as a Bolshevik, Stalin had operated in the violent Georgian underworld, and had been involved in illegal activities such as bank robberies.

herself in the family flat whilst Stalin was at a party. Stalin was deeply disturbed, and whilst recovering outwardly, many of his more extreme personality traits came to the fore from this time onwards.

Leader of the terror State

As explained earlier, Stalin used the Kirov assassination to implement the first large-scale purge of the 1930s. His personal role was crucial, although so-called revisionist historians have tended to downplay this aspect and focused on other factors as driving the purges forward. John Arch Getty was the first notable historian to argue the limited extent of Stalin's personal role (*The Origins of the Great Purges*, 1985).

A closer look

The 'revisionist' approach to Stalin's role in the terror

'Revisionists' is the label widely used to describe historians who challenge long-established interpretations.

Revisionists queried the extent of Stalin's involvement in the Kirov murder, and pointed out that after the initial backlash, the situation quietened for a while, suggesting that Stalin's response may not have been pre-planned. The historian Getty argued that, although Stalin was at the centre of power, the regime was not that efficient, and could not even ensure that orders from Moscow were carried out in the provinces. Certain individuals such as Molotov and Zhdanov, who held important positions and were close to Stalin, were prepared to argue policy with him, whilst the NKVD sometimes acted as a law unto itself. Therefore Stalin was not in complete, unquestioned control.

However, the key question must be: how much control did Stalin actually have? He must have known most of what was going on. He ran his own personal spy system or 'special section' that kept close tabs on various party leaders. The Politburo rarely met, and Stalin operated largely on a one-to-one basis with his ministers, who were therefore often isolated and at odds with each other. Even though there is some evidence of disagreements amongst leading Communists on various policies, such as the pace of industrialisation, it would have been unlikely and certainly very dangerous for any grouping to have emerged to challenge Stalin. It may well be true that Stalin, in encouraging the purges, did not have a precise plan about where they might lead. However, when he decided to call a halt to the bloodletting, at least temporarily, it was clear that he was in charge and his will was obeyed – witness the treatment of Yezhov.

Cross-reference

For details on the treatment of Yezhov under Stalin see pages 95–6.

Fig. 7 *By order of Stalin, the Communist Party is being 'purged' of members who do not see eye to eye with the Red rulers. Here is one of Stalin's purge committees at work, 1 May 1933*

Overall, historians' interpretations of the terror can be divided roughly into four categories:

1   The view that State violence was an integral part of the Soviet system. After all, the Bolsheviks had not been voted into power in 1917. They had seized power by force and then used force to maintain

Activity

Revision exercise

Construct a simple chart and find at least two pieces of evidence both in support of, and to contradict, each of the four interpretations of the terror outlined above.

themselves in power. Any means were justified in order to ensure that the first Socialist State remained intact in the face of a hostile world. Therefore Stalin's terror was in essence a continuation of Lenin's terror. Although Stalin's contribution was on a much larger scale, the essential ingredients had already been there from the revolution onwards: witness Lenin's creation of the Cheka; the brutal suppression of the Kronstadt Mutiny; the imprisonment or execution of political opponents. There were plenty of precedents for what Stalin did.

2 The view that Stalin's terror was very unique in its motives and scope, and that Stalin was very much at the hub of events. He was personally responsible for promoting and then ending the purges.

3 The view that other leading party members, communist organisations and local party activists played an equally important part in promoting the terror, confident that this is what their leader wanted, or else they had their own motives and were confident that there would be no check from the centre.

4 The view that although particular individuals, including of course Stalin, played an important role in the progress of the terror, it also accelerated in scope and extent because of unplanned factors. It almost took on a life of its own. For example, the terror could be used by individuals to settle personal scores, or to get rid of rivals and so open avenues of promotion to enthusiastic activists. Fear fed on fear. If you were in fear of being denounced, it might be better to prove your loyalty by denouncing someone else first.

Many Soviet citizens apparently believed the official party line that Stalin was a heroic leader, protecting his people from a nest of traitors trying to hold back Soviet progress or even destroy the country. Many anxious about excesses during the terror could even persuade themselves that Stalin was not personally responsible or possibly did not even know about them. However, there were some individuals in no doubt of Stalin's role and who were prepared to say so. Early on in the terror, in 1933, Osip Mandelstam wrote *The Stalin Epigram* (Source 9):

Exploring the detail

Mandelstam wrote this poem (Source 9) in 1935, read it to some friends, was denounced to the authorities and exiled for three years – a light sentence, possibly because Stalin loved poetry. However, he was re-arrested and died in a labour camp in 1938.

Activity

Source analysis

Read the poem in Source 9.

1 Explain the references to 'Kremlin mountaineer' and 'The murderer and peasant-slayer'.

2 What do you think is the overall message of this poem?

We live, deaf to the land beneath us,
Ten steps away no one hears our speeches,

All we hear is the Kremlin mountaineer,
The murderer and peasant-slayer.

His fingers are fat as grubs
And the words, final as lead weights, fall from his lips,

His cockroach whiskers leer
And his boot tops gleam.

Around him a rabble of thin-necked leaders-
Fawning half-men for him to play with.

They whinny, purr or whine
As he prates and points a finger

One by one forging his laws, to be flung
Like horseshoes at the head, to the eye of the groin.

And every killing is a treat
For the broad-chested Ossete*

9   *Mandelstam, The Stalin Epigram, 1933
A reference to rumours of Stalin's supposed Persian ancestry

Contrast Mandelstam's poem with these excerpts taken from Bedny, D. (1937) *We dealt the enemy a cruel counterblow* (Source 10):

> Monstrous! I can hardly put in words
>
> That thing my head can find no place for
>
> For which no name would do, such an awful evil.
>
> How despicable is the hissing voice of spies!
>
> How disgraceful the sight of enemies among us!
>
> Shame to the mothers that gave birth
>
> To these dogs of unprecedented foulness!
>
> The poison oozes from their fascist gut.
>
> When they stuck their snouts in the fascist trough,
>
> They meant to bring misfortune to their homeland!
>
> A nest of spies has been uncovered!
>
> Unmasking them was fortunate for us:
>
> What a joy to realise that we dealt
>
> The enemy camp a cruel counterblow!
>
> Nary an ash will remain of these loathsome vermin.
>
> The Soviet land has grown, gained strength, and flourished
>
> In defiance of its evil foes.
>
> Didn't we study in the school of Lenin?
>
> Heading with Stalin toward our radiant destiny,
>
> Standing together in our unconquerable will,
>
> We will arrive at worldwide victory.
>
> And none of these damned traitors will bar the way!

10   *Excerpts from **We dealt the enemy a cruel counterblow** by Bedny, 1937*

Stalin himself did not try to escape responsibility for the purges, but justified them, using the euphemism 'cleansing'. He told the 18th Party Congress in March 1939 (Source 11):

> It cannot be said that the cleansings were not accompanied by grave mistakes, more than might have been expected. Undoubtedly, we shall have no further need to resort to the method of mass cleansings. Nevertheless, the cleansings were unavoidable and their results, on the whole, were beneficial.

11   *Taken from a speech made by Stalin*

Key personnel and the instruments of terror

Apart from Stalin himself, there were several individuals and organisations with a significant role in the terror.

Fig. 8 *Karl Sobelson, known as Karl Radek (1885–1939). Soviet politician of Polish origin. One of those tried and executed*

■ Exploring the detail

The argument that the USSR had become a 'bureaucratic State' under Stalin was a common criticism made by his opponents like Trotsky. It implied that the party and State had combined into a stifling, oppressive, huge administrative machine whose main function seemed to be to perpetuate itself rather than develop a society really geared to the needs of the people. Far from being revolutionary, the party had become resistant to real change. Critics of Stalin compared this situation to revolutionary France, which had given rise to Napoleon Bonaparte. He had risen to power during the revolution and then became an emperor and champion of law and order, destroying what critics saw as the gains of the revolution.

■ Activity

Talking point

Use the following two questions as the basis for a group or class discussion.

1 What truth was there in Trotsky's accusations and his criticism of the USSR under Stalin?

2 Based on your knowledge of Trotsky's career, do you think the USSR would have been a different place if Trotsky rather than Stalin had become leader?

■ Cross-reference

For more about Zinoviev, Kamenev and Bukharin in the 1920s, see pages 12–3, 15–7, and 20–1.

Trotsky: the absent bogeyman

During the terror Trotsky was in exile abroad, as he had been since he lost his influence in the USSR in the late-1930s. He had maintained a high profile with a constant output of writings justifying his past behaviour and criticising the development of the Soviet State under Stalin. Despite Trotsky's physical absence from the USSR, he played an important part in the terror, albeit unwittingly. Accused of being a 'Trotskyite' was a convenient label to stick on anyone whom Stalin and the authorities wanted to persecute. Soviet propaganda claimed that Trotskyite 'spies, saboteurs and wreckers' were active throughout the USSR trying to undermine the progress towards Socialism. Ironically, one of Trotsky's weaknesses in the 1920s was precisely that he had not had a strong party base inside the USSR. Whilst he may have had some old sympathisers inside the USSR in the 1930s, Trotskyite 'influence' was almost certainly exaggerated for political effect. Nevertheless, his reputation made him a possible rallying point for anti-Stalinists abroad, and in exile Trotsky continued to irritate the Stalinist regime with his analysis of what was going on inside the USSR. In *The Revolution Betrayed*, Trotsky wrote of the 'rapid degeneration' of the Communist Party. Stalin's regime, 'resting upon a police and officers' corps, and allowing of no control whatever, is obviously a variant of Bonapartism.' In other words, just as Napoleon had brought the French Revolution to an end, Stalin had perverted and destroyed the gains of the Russian Revolution and created a bureaucratic State. Instead of the Communist Party running the State for the benefit of the people, the State was preoccupied with preserving and extending its own power. Trotsky wrote that:

> The chief merit of a Bolshevik was declared to be obedience. Revolutionaries were replaced by professional functionaries [i.e. administrators], whilst Stalin is the personification of the bureaucracy.

Stalin would not let this pass. Stalinist agents sought out Trotsky, and he was eventually murdered in Mexico in 1940.

Kamenev, Zinoviev and Bukharin: victims of old rivalries

These three men had been prominent Communists in the 1920s. Having been defeated by Stalin in the power struggle to succeed Lenin and in the arguments about the next phase of post-NEP Russia, Zinoviev, Kamenev and Bukharin had to all intents and purposes drifted into insignificance by the mid-1930s. But not as far as Stalin was concerned. Did he fear their influence, or was he really bent on revenge for perceived insults and their temerity in opposing him years before? Certainly, their naivety was painfully evident when set alongside Stalin's ruthlessness.

Having been defeated by Stalin in the policy arguments and struggle for influence in the late-1920s, these once influential Old Bolsheviks had admitted the 'errors of their ways' and accepted their demotion. They then made the mistake of believing that they were safe.

Kamenev and Zinoviev (along with Yagoda, the secret police chief) were arrested after the Kirov affair. After their Show Trials, confessions and sentences, Kamenev met his death, by shooting, with dignity; Zinoviev with panic and despair. For Stalin's entertainment, his security chief later mimicked the victim's last desperate moments before execution. Bukharin pleaded in vain by letter to Stalin for an alternative to execution, such as exile to America, where he promised he 'would smash Trotsky's face in'.

Some other victims

There were many prominent victims of the terror, including some whom Stalin had known well for years. The following were just two of many victims.

Ordzhonikidze

Ordzhonikidze was the Commissar for Heavy Industry and objected to excessive use of terror. Stalin had his deputy shot. Ordzhonikidze possibly saw what was coming, and is believed to have committed suicide in 1937, although officially he died of a heart attack.

Nestor Lakoba

Lakoba was the first of Stalin's immediate circle to be killed. An old associate of Stalin, and a party leader in the Caucasus, his power was usurped by Beria. Lakoba made the mistake of refusing Stalin's offer of the leadership of the NKVD – soon afterwards in 1936 he died of a 'heart attack' after a meal at Beria's apartment, exclaiming, 'the snake Beria has killed me'. It was impossible to prove poisoning because Beria had his organs removed. After his death, Lakoba was declared 'an enemy of the people'. His widow was tortured to death, his mother beaten to death, and his children imprisoned until Beria had them tortured and killed.

The chief purgers

Three leaders of the security services served Stalin loyally during the 1930s terror, but all became victims themselves.

Genrikh (Henry) Yagoda

Yagoda, trained originally as a statistician and a chemist's assistant, joined the Cheka and became a Stalin supporter in 1929. He created the slave labour camp complex that was an important part of the industrialisation programme. His personal hobbies were gardening and pornography. Yagoda organised the 1936 Show Trials but fell out of favour with Stalin and ended up on trial himself.

At his trial in 1938, Yagoda denied being a spy or being involved in Kirov's murder, although he did admit to other 'heinous crimes'. He was accused, amongst other things, of having tried to poison his successor Yezhov and the writer Maxim Gorky, and assassinating Kirov. Yagoda was shot in 1938, possibly by his own successor Yezhov. Yagoda's family members were shot, imprisoned or exiled. Yagoda's removal ensured that Stalin had full control of the NKVD.

Nikolai Yezhov

Yezhov gave his name to the period of the Great Terror, still known in popular memory as the 'Yezhovshchina', in reference to his time in charge of the NKVD (September 1936 to December 1938). The 'bloody dwarf' (he was unusually short) was originally popular and was Stalin's protégé, called by him 'my Blackberry'. He was regarded as intelligent, hard working and loyal. He was also a tension-riddled, alcoholic, drug-addicted, deviant, who personally supervised torture after being put in charge of the NKVD. He was in charge of the massive expansion of the terror. Yezhov openly admitted that the terror was entirely random in its operation, declaring:

> We are launching a major attack on the Enemy; let there be no resentment if we bump someone with an elbow. Better that ten innocent people should suffer than one spy get away. When you chop wood, chips fly.

In 1939, when Stalin wished to end the terror, Yezhov was quietly removed from office and shot, being made a scapegoat for the excesses of the purges.

Just before his fall, during the terror, a renowned Kazhak folk poet, Dzhambul Dzhabaev, published a poem about Yezhov including the lines (Source 12):

> In a flash of lightning we came to know you
>
> The hero Yezhov was nurtured for battle
>
> In the wisdom and words of the Great Lenin.
>
> Yezhov heard with his heart, heard with his blood
>
> The fiery summons of the Great Stalin.
>
> He saddled his steed and rode off to the front.
>
> Class struggled with class. The land was ablaze.
>
> The blood of the motherland flowed in those days.
>
> The enemy squeezed us tight in its ring
>
> Of iron and steel, fire and lead.
>
> The Trotskyist bands of spies crept up on us,
>
> And the Bukharinites, those cunning swamp snakes.
>
> But they fell into the traps of Yezhov,
>
> Devoted friend of the mighty Stalin.
>
> Yezhov destroyed their traitorous ring.
>
> The scorpion brood was entirely crushed
>
> By the hands of Yezhov – the hands of the people.
>
> You are a sword, bared calmly and fiercely,
>
> A fire that burns out the nests of the snakes.
>
> Thank you, Yezhov, that you beat the alarm
>
> As you stand on guard for your nation and leader.

12　　　　　　　　　　　　　　*Published in **Pravda**, December 1937*

Activity

Talking point

Use these two questions as the basis for a class discussion.

1 What is the message of the poem in Source 12?

2 How effective is it as propaganda?

Fig. 9 *Lavrenti Beria photographed in 1953 was the head of the Russian secret service from 1938–53 and nearly succeeded in establishing himself as dictator upon Stalin's death. Beria was shot in the Lubyanka prison in Moscow*

Lavrenti Beria

Like Stalin, a Georgian, and at least his equal in ruthlessness, Beria had probably been a double agent before becoming a Chekist. Intelligent and calculating, Beria wormed his way into Stalin's favour, working his way up to replace Yezhov as head of the secret police. Beria's motto was 'In order to survive, always strike first'. Feared at least as much as Stalin, Beria was utterly brutal and sadistic. He had a particular interest in the use of poisons. Beria threatened colleagues, personally tortured suspects, and abducted and raped countless women, often the wives of colleagues or unknown women seized off the streets. Yet he slightly improved conditions in the Gulag camps, not out of humanity but because he reasoned that inmates who were better treated would be more productive for the economy. After Stalin's death and Beria's own arrest, his former officers fought for the privilege of shooting him.

A closer look

The instruments of terror: the security forces

The USSR was a police State, relying for conformity from the population not just through patriotism, apathy, ambition and propaganda, but through a network of police forces, party activists and informers. The most powerful and feared instrument of terror was the NKVD, direct descendants of Lenin's security service.

The Soviet internal security forces

1917–22 **Cheka** (All-Russian Extraordinary Commission for Combating Counter-revolution and Sabotage). Lenin's 'sharp sword of the revolution', set up to ensure Bolshevik survival during the Civil War from 1918, with wide powers to deal with any real or potential opposition.

1922–34 **GPU**, then **OGPU** (Department of Political Police).

1934–43 **NKVD** (People's Commissariat of Internal Affairs), led in turn by Yagoda, Yezhov and Beria. Given extraordinary powers to carry out the purges. The importance of 1934 was that in that year the ordinary police was also unified under the NKVD, and the national network of labour camps (Gulag) was also set up under the NKVD. Therefore the whole system of policing and State repression was unified under one body. In 1938, the use of torture, only officially allowed in 1937, was reduced and in theory, although often not in practice, proper investigative procedures were re-introduced to deal with suspects.

Fig. 10 *An anti-Soviet French cartoon (Courtesy of John laver)*

ЕСЛИ ЗАВТРА ВОЙНА, ЕСЛИ ВРАГ НАПАДЕТ, ЕСЛИ ТЕМНАЯ СИЛА НАГРЯНЕТ, КАК ОДИН ЧЕЛОВЕК, ВЕСЬ СОВЕТСКИЙ НАРОД ЗА СВОБОДНУЮ РОДИНУ ВСТАНЕТ!

Fig. 11 *A Soviet poster showing the Red Army stoutly defending the USSR against a brutal fascist enemy (Courtesy of John Laver)*

Activity

Source analysis

Consider Figure 11 and Sources 13 and 14.

1 Explain how the views in Source 13 support or challenge those in Source 14 about the motives for the terror.

2 Use Figure 11, Sources 13 and 14 and your own knowledge.

'The Great Terror in the 1930s USSR was designed to strengthen Stalin's personal dictatorship rather than benefit the country over which he ruled.' Explain why you agree or disagree with this view. (This could be done as a class debate.)

[Stalin mused] …The history of mankind was the history of its leaders. The spirit of an age was determined by the man who made the age himself. All opponents, past, present and future, had to be liquidated. The sole socialist country in the world could survive only if it were unshakeably stable. The state must be strong in case of war; the state must be mighty if it wants peace. It must be feared. In order to turn a peasant society into an industrialised country, countless material and human sacrifices were necessary. The people would have to be forced to accept the sacrifice. This could not be achieved by enthusiasm alone. An authority that inspired fear was necessary. If a few million people had to perish in the process, history would forgive Comrade Stalin. All great rulers had been harsh. Sending Trotsky into exile out of the country had been a humane act, and therefore a mistaken one. He would not send Zinoviev and Kamenev into exile abroad. They would serve as the first foundation stone of the bastion of fear he must build in order to defend the country.

13   *Adapted from A. Rybakov, **Children of the Arbat**, 1989*

Rybakov's hard-hitting novel about the terror was suppressed in the USSR for 20 years before being published in Britain in 1988, because it was considered too politically sensitive in the USSR.

Obviously Stalin could not control everything – an absurd proposition given the country's size, the upheavals of the economic revolution and the clear weakness of the party-state machine. Stalin probably could not even control everything happening in the central committee. But he could control what happened to the Old Bolsheviks. It is inconceivable that the show trials occurred without his active consent. As for the military purge, despite the possibility of Nazi intrigue inside the USSR, the notion that Stalin destroyed the officers lest they turn against the regime therefore remains the most plausible explanation. Even if the Yezhovschina (the Great Terror Years) was a unique event, arising from several factors, it was Stalin who tipped the balance in Yezhov's favour. It is difficult to imagine that a politician as astute as Stalin did not anticipate at least some of what was to follow, if only because the power of the secret police had been growing steadily.

14   *Adapted from C. Ward, **Stalin's Russia**, 1993*

Summary questions

1 How important was the Kirov assassination for Stalin?

2 Explain why so many 'Old Bolsheviks' were purged.

3 Explain why the army was purged.

4 Explain why the Show Trials were set up.

8   The impact of the terror to 1941

Fig. 1 *Stalin and his companions. Satirical cartoon in the newspaper* Aux Ecoutes, *1938*

Activity

Thinking point

Do you agree with Stalin?

One of Stalin's colleagues asked him whether he would rather people followed him out of conviction or fear. To his surprise, Stalin replied 'Fear'. When asked to explain, Stalin replied, 'People are always afraid. But convictions can change.'

The impact of the terror on the party, the armed services and the Soviet population as a whole

The scope of the terror

Although the Show Trials of 1936–8 received considerable publicity, the number of victims involved in them was relatively small compared to the millions of less-prominent Soviet citizens who suffered much less publicly in these years. This is true even if the millions of peasants displaced, imprisoned or killed during the struggle over collectivisation during the early 1930s are taken out of the equation.

The pace of arrests increased considerably in 1937 when the government issued a decree condemning 'anti-Soviet elements' in the USSR. Yezhov drew up arrest lists that included people in industry and a wide range of professions, including historians. Arrest quotas were applied to each district and each public organisation, and the one requirement was to fulfil the quotas, regardless of whether any charges against suspects were credible or not. The quotas included numbers to be shot, and numbers to be sent to labour camps. Many officials were denounced, but thousands of ordinary people were also swept up in arrests. Sometimes there were large numbers arrested from individual factories or other institutions. Over 1,000 people were arrested from one factory alone.

Relatives, family members and friends of those initially arrested were also liable to be rounded up. A historian of the terror, Robert Conquest, recorded that in Odessa one Communist denounced 230 people, whilst in Poltava another denounced his entire local party organisation.

Confessions were often extracted from victims by threats or physical and mental torture. One common practice was the 'conveyor belt system' whereby a victim was passed from one interrogator to another until he or she was mentally or physically broken.

There were occasionally signs of opposition to Stalin at this time, but very few. In June 1937, a prominent member of the Central Committee, Pyatnitsky, spoke out against the physical elimination of Bukharin and his colleagues, and against giving Yezhov extraordinary powers. On the following morning Yezhov 'unearthed' evidence that Pyatnitsky had been an agent of the tsarist secret police, and the Committee passed a vote of no confidence in him. It is also known that during 1937–8, up to 74 military officials were shot for refusing to approve the execution of people whom they believed innocent.

Fig. 2 *Political trial in Moscow. Nikolai Krylenko (far left), Commissar of Justice. The next year, Krylenko 'disappeared', 1936*

Exploring the detail

The impact of the terror on Communist Party membership

By the time of the 1939 Party Congress, 1,108 of the 1,966 delegates to the 1934 Party Congress had been arrested. Less than two per cent of the 1934 delegates actually attended the 1939 Party Congress.

In 1939, only 16 out of the 71 members of the 1934 Central Committee were still free citizens.

Party membership fell by 36 per cent between 1934 and 1939.

According to the Russian author Sakharov, more than 1.2 million party members, half the total membership, were arrested in 1936–9. He estimated that 600,000 party members were executed. Party membership records were not kept efficiently and are therefore unreliable.

The impact of the terror on the Communist Party

In January 1928, there were approximately 1.25 million full and candidate members of the Communist Party in the USSR. (Candidate members were hopeful new members who had to serve an apprenticeship period before full admittance to the party.) By January 1933, this figure had grown to 3.5 million, mainly because the implementation of the Five Year Plan required many more trusty administrators. However, such a rapid growth in party membership inevitably meant that many new members did not come up to scratch. Consequently, from 1929, there were frequent expulsions from the party for failings such as 'passivity', 'lack of discipline' and 'drunkenness'. In 1933, 800,000 members were expelled, and 340,000 in 1934. Total membership had fallen to 2,350,000 by 1935, and the bulk of those expelled were newer recruits. Recruitment to the party was actually suspended between 1933 and 1936. Therefore the party was already concerned about the membership long before the onset of the worst period of the terror.

What was significant about the nature of the purges against the party was that:

- between 1933 and 1936 action against party membership was officially organised by the party organisation, and aimed specifically at those party members deemed falling short of the standard expected.

- between 1936 and 1938 (when actually fewer members were expelled – 850,000 as opposed to over 1 million) – action was 'unofficial' in that it was not authorised by the Central Committee, but was privately dictated by Stalin and his NKVD under Yezhov. The intention was mainly to make the party a compliant tool of Stalin.

- by 1939 less than 10 per cent of the party membership had joined before 1920. Overall less than one quarter of recruits since 1920 survived the purges.

- whereas in the early years of the USSR preference in membership was given to working-class recruits, during the later 1930s recruits came from a much wider range, and included large numbers of technical specialists and people from an administrative or 'intellectual' background. The party put artists and writers on a pedestal and awarded them privileges and honours if they toed the party line. But as a group, the party distrusted 'intellectuals', because they might be people who thought a lot, and thought for themselves, which was always dangerous for a totalitarian regime that wanted to mould people into a particular way of thinking. The party was less concerned with its members having the right political credentials, but with meeting the needs of a developing economy. The party became younger and included more better educated members. It was still predominantly male, with only 14.9 per cent of members being female by 1941.

- the party leadership was less affected by the terror than is often supposed. Several of the prominent victims like Zinoviev, Kamenev and Bukharin had already lost power and influence in the USSR. Several 'old Stalinists' – for example Molotov, Kalinin, Mikoyan, Kaganovich and Voroshilov, were still in the leadership after 1939. They had already been important in the party before Stalin's rise, although, crucially, they remained totally loyal to Stalin throughout this period. In the 1939 Politburo, there were only three men – Khrushchev, Zhdanov and Beria – who had been promoted by Stalin.

- although the expulsion of many party members was a major development, it should be emphasised that expulsion did not

Fig. 3 *Soviet politician Mikhail Ivanovitch Kalinin (1875–1946), with Voroshilov and Mikoyan, 1926*

necessarily mean arrest, imprisonment or death, although that was the fate of many individuals. Possibly of greater impact was the loss not of bureaucrats and administrators but the loss of experienced army officers, teachers, engineers and specialists. Many of these were not necessarily party members, but their contribution was vital to the development of the country in the long run.

Fig. 4 *At the court of justice of the Moscow district, they are waiting for their turn, c.1930*

Few party members were prepared to stand up to the regime, even when they had doubts. This is scarcely surprising given that most of their leaders were themselves fearful of the likely consequences of disagreeing with Stalin. Stalin frequently humiliated even members of the Politburo. One Soviet historian recorded that Stalin used to insult Beria, strike him and throw tea at him. Several family members of leading Communists were imprisoned: for example the wife of Kalinin, the Soviet President, carried out heavy labour in a Gulag camp between 1938 and 1945. Molotov was a very strong character and regarded by many as second only to Stalin, but even he stopped pleading the case of his own imprisoned wife. Molotov's daughter declared that she had no mother when she applied to join the party.

The impact of the terror on the armed forces

The Red Army was just under 1 million strong in 1936, and this figure had increased to 5 million by 1941. The five-year expansion period involved not just an increase in numbers but a reorganisation of structure and an adaptation to new weapons such as tanks and rockets. These sorts of changes were also taking place in some other European armies. What was different about the USSR was that the changes were accompanied by the terror. The impact of the terror on the army has sometimes been overestimated. Probably up to 23,000 officers were shot or dismissed (others were later reinstated). The great majority of those purged were not killed. However, a quarter of a million new officers would have had to be recruited just to match the increase in troops taking place in this period. It was a major task to find and train this number of officers whatever the political situation, and the lack of experience evident in the first months of the war in 1941 can only very partially be put down to the purges.

■ A closer look

Stalin's view of politics and morality

Stalin frequently made notes and comments in the margins of the many books he read. We know that he read the book *The Tale of the Zealous Leader* by Mikhail Saltykov-Shchedrin, and Stalin underlined parts of the text as in this extract.

There were two guiding rules. One: the more harm a leader does, the more good he does for the fatherland. If he abolishes learning, good, if he burns down a city, good; if he terrifies the population, even better... Two: to have as many bastards as possible to do your bidding...

Then [the leader] gathered the 'bastards' and said to them: 'Bastards, write denunciations!'... They write denunciations, draw up harmful plans... And all this semi-literate stinking matter gets to the zealous leader's office...

[The leader] gathered the 'bastards' and said: 'Tell me, bastards, what do you think real harm consists of?'

And the bastards replied unaminously... 'The harm we bastards do should count as good; and good, if done by anyone else, count as harm. That nobody should dare to say a word about us bastards, while we bastards can yap what we like about whomever we want to.'

What conclusions about Stalin's attitude towards ruling the USSR can you draw from this extract?

Nevertheless, at the time, the purge of the military was regarded as very significant. Marshall Tukhachevsky had been an innovative, modernising general who thought carefully about improving military tactics. He and other leading generals were arrested, convicted of treason and spying, and shot in 1937. Tukhachevsky had once been close to Trotsky, which by itself would have aroused Stalin's suspicions. He died protesting his loyalty to Stalin. In 1957, a Soviet military court found no evidence of treason and Tukhachevsky's reputation was rehabilitated. It is clear that the generals were tortured into confessions. Tukhachevsky's confession document admitting to conspiring with Trotsky is stained with his blood, following a week of beatings by his interrogators. The NKVD investigators received medals. Yezhov was the prime mover in constructing a case that Tukhachevsky and other military leaders were planning a military coup against Stalin and the government. It is not clear whether Stalin was also initiating events or whether he was reacting to Yezhov's 'evidence'. The whole affair was clouded because there is other evidence that the Germans were involved in planting evidence to implicate the Red Army in a plot and thereby prompt Stalin into a damaging overreaction. Molotov was convinced for years afterwards that the evidence produced by the NKVD against the generals was genuine and that there was a military plot to put Stalin on trial or shoot him outright. It was not difficult to be suspicious: since 1922 Red Army officers had been working with German officers on tactics and ideology. Russian officers had worked abroad as military attaches – which, to a paranoid leader, was tantamount to spying.

The impact of the terror on the ordinary soldier was probably no greater or less than on many other sectors of the population. What was more significant was the lack of experience of their leaders: about three-quarters of officers and political officers had been in post for less than one year, and this problem was made worse by the failure of the political leadership to defend the USSR effectively in the first months of the forthcoming war against Germany. This was the result of Stalin's decision to create a new army 'cleansed of rotten gangrene down to the healthy flesh'. As Richard Overy concluded: 'The crisis was used to restore political domination over the Soviet armed forces at the expense of the military modernisers' (*The Dictators*, 2005).

Exploring the detail

Both Russia and Germany had been defeated in the First World War. In 1922, in the Treaty of Rapallo, they secretly agreed to support each other in military training. Hitler ended this agreement after he came to power in 1933, but contacts between the two countries' military forces remained.

The impact of the terror on the Soviet population

Estimates vary considerably, but they suggest broadly that during the Yezhov years (September 1936 to December 1938) over 7 million people were arrested, and over 1 million executed.

Fig. 5 *Sergei Korolkoff's pictures depict the fate of those sent by Beria's organisation to 'corrective' labour camps. 'Members of all races, within the Soviet Union, they go, some for many years, to work in woods, mines and factories'*

Between 1936 and 1939, 10 to 15 million may have died, from torture, execution, exile or in camps. These figures do not include the millions who died during the collectivisation famine. Robert Conquest (*The Great Terror*, 1971) calculated that of those arrested and sent to camps during 1936–8, possibly less than 10 per cent survived.

However, the KGB's own estimates (made public after 1990) tend to be much lower than earlier estimates by Soviet and Western historians alike. The official figures of those investigated by the secret police, according to a report prepared for Stalin's successors in 1953, were as shown in Table 1.

Table 1 *The KGB's estimates of people investigated by the secret police*

Year	All crimes	Counter-revolutionary crimes	Convictions	Executions
1934	205,173	90,417	78,999	2,056
1935	193,083	108,935	267,076	1,229
1936	131,168	91,127	274,670	1,118
1937	936,750	779,056	790,665	353,074
1938	638,509	593,326	554,258	328,618
Total for 1937–8	1,575,259	1,372,382	1,344,923	681,692

Activity

Talking point

Study the figures in Table 1.

1. What trends do the figures show, and can you explain them?

2. How would you account for differences in the 'official' and 'unofficial' figures for victims of the terror?

Targets for executions and exiles were set by the authorities, and varied from region to region. The areas most targeted were the Moscow and

Leningrad regions, and western Siberia (which was thought to be the centre of a military plot against the regime).

There is controversy not just about the numbers who were purged (either imprisoned or killed), but about the impact of the terror on those left living and at liberty. There is some evidence that many ordinary people were less traumatised than is commonly imagined, as Source 1 from a foreign worker suggests:

> Chaos reigned in the Magnitogorsk Plant. A foreman would come to work in the morning and say to his men, 'Now today we must do this and that.' The workers would sneer at him and say, 'Go on! You're a wrecker yourself. Tomorrow they'll come and arrest you. All you engineers and technicians are wreckers.'

1 *J. Scott, **Behind the Urals: An American Worker in Russia's City of Steel**, 1973*

Activity

Thinking point

Groups that suffered proportionally highly during the purges (discounting the peasantry in the early 1930s, who suffered terribly from persecution and famine) included: urban dwellers; educated classes; regional bureaucrats; the military; the intelligentsia; enterprise managers; and priests.

Can you think why these groups in particular bore the brunt of the purges?

One of Russia's greatest poets, Anna Akhmatova, recalled these years in which she and her family personally suffered (Source 2).

> **1 April 1957**
>
> In the awful years of Yezhovian horror, I spent seventeen months standing in line in front of various prisons in Leningrad. One day someone 'recognised' me. Then a woman with blue lips, who was standing behind me, and who, of course, had never heard my name, came out of the stupor which typified all of us, and whispered into my ear (everyone there spoke only in whispers):
>
> Can you describe this?
>
> And I said:
>
> I can.
>
> Then something like a fleeting smile passed over what once had been her face.
>
> **Introduction (1935)**
>
> This happened when only the dead wore smiles –
>
> They rejoiced at being safe from harm.
>
> And Leningrad dangled from its jails
>
> Like some unnecessary arm.
>
> And when the hosts of those convicted,
>
> Marched by – mad, tormented throngs,
>
> And train whistles were restricted
>
> To singing separation songs.
>
> The stars of death stood overhead,
>
> And guiltless Russia, that pariah,
>
> Writhed under boots, all blood-be'spattered,
>
> And the wheels of many a black maria.

2 *From the poem sequence **Requiem***

The experiences of the victims

Torture

Torture was used widely by the lower ranks of the NKVD to extract confessions: both psychological and all manner of physical tortures. Most of the police were poorly educated and poorly trained, and willing to obey arbitrary orders. Often they did not need to wait for orders at all, but took matters into their own hands. Leading figures, including Beria himself, sometimes took part in torturing suspects personally. Beria often used a blackjack or truncheon as a weapon. He boasted of his victims: 'Let me have one night with him and I'll have him confessing he's the King of England.'

Use of informers

Informers were certainly used to back up the police, although estimates vary considerably. In cities such as Moscow there may have been several informers in one building. However, other estimates suggest a figure of approximately one informer to every 400 people, a far smaller proportion than used for example by the communist regime in East Germany after 1949.

Crimes

The NKVD was particularly keen to root out those considered dangerous to society, such as those belonging to 'suspect groups' like 'gypsies' or former members of other political parties. Often the police were simply desperate to fulfil targets. Many arrests arose out of denunciations or personal tensions between individuals. People were often arrested simply because they were relatives, workmates or friends of those already arrested. However, despite popular belief, the terror was often resisted successfully: there are many examples of people successfully defending themselves against accusations, and sometimes their friends or colleagues successfully defended them and charges were dropped.

The labour camps

Forced labour had been used as a form of punishment since 1918, and labour camps were built from the early 1920s. However, 1937 was a key year when:

> Soviet camps temporarily transformed themselves from indifferently managed prisons in which people died by accident, into genuinely deadly camps where prisoners were deliberately worked to death, or actually murdered, in far larger numbers than they had been in the past.
>
> *A. Applebaum, Gulag: A History, 2003*

Many of the camp commandants themselves were purged. The term 'political prisoner' increasingly gave way in 1937 to the term 'enemy of the people', a phrase first used by Lenin in 1917, and then used by Stalin in 1927 to describe Trotsky and his followers. An 'enemy of the people' did not have to openly profess his crime: according to Beria, 'An enemy of the people is not only one who commits sabotage, but one who doubts the rightness of the party line.' Such 'enemies' were no longer regarded as citizens and were not granted the few occasional privileges given to camp inmates before the Great Terror. Gulag prisoners were no longer regarded as capable of 're-education', and there was no longer the possibility of early release for good behaviour.

A closer look

The Kolyma camps

One of the most notorious camps in the Gulag was the Kolyma Camp in the north-east corner of Siberia. The Kolyma region is rich in mineral resources, especially gold, but is one of the most inhospitable parts of the world. Temperatures for much of the winter are as low as minus 45 degrees centigrade. It was a three-month trip by train and boat for prisoners to reach the camps in Kolyma. Stalin needed the gold to exchange directly with the Western world for technology and machinery. By 1932 there were nearly 10,000 prisoners working there, including many former engineers and other specialists. The death rate amongst prisoners was high, although conditions in the camp improved slightly as the authorities were anxious to extract valuable resources and not just punish or kill off prisoners. Prisoners who worked well – 'shock-workers' – could earn privileges. Prisoners worked not just in the camps but built roads, docks and even the city of Magadan.

One Kolyma survivor, Varlam Shalamov, wrote a graphic account of camp life in *Kolyma Tales*. It was a constant struggle for survival, as professional criminals dominated the camps and bullied other inmates unmercifully in order to increase their own chances of survival (Source 3):

The evil acts committed by criminals in camp are innumerable. The unfortunates are those from whom the thief steals their last rags, confiscates their last coin. The working man is afraid to complain, for he sees that the criminals are stronger than the camp authorities… Tens of thousands of people have been beaten to death by thieves.

3
*V. Shalamov, **Kolyma Tales***

Another inmate wrote of a meeting with a Kolyma thief who described one of the hazards of camp life (Source 4):

I was playing cards and I lost. I had no cash… Our council of senior prisoners met to hand out my punishment. The plaintiff [the man who was owed the money] wanted all my left-hand fingers off. The council offered two. They bargained a bit and agreed on three. So I put my hand on the table and the man I'd lost to took a stick and with five strokes knocked off my three fingers.

4
*A. Applebaum, **Gulag: A History**, 2003*

Life in the camps was hard, but conditions did vary considerably from camp to camp. Older camps tended to be better run than the new ones opened in 1937–8. Siberian gold mines were the worst. The further a camp was from civilisation, the worst the conditions often were. Political prisoners were often treated worse than 'ordinary' criminals. Conditions in the camps were generally at their worst in the Yezhov years, and improved under Beria, who saw the economic benefits of a more orderly regime. However, the type of task provided for forced labour, the conditions for the inmates, and the resources devoted to running the camp system, make it very unlikely that the camp system made a positive contribution to the Soviet economy. This was never the main intention, especially after the expansion of the terror in the 1930s.

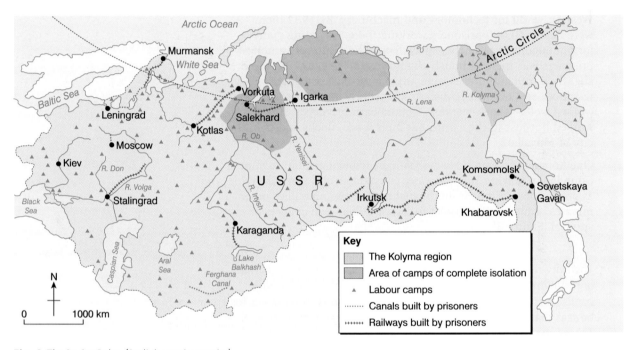

Fig. 6 *The Soviet Gulag (Stalin's convict empire)*

Ordinary people

Although many people suffered unjustly during the terror, it is possible to exaggerate its effects on ordinary people. Until well into 1937, it was members of the USSR's elite that were in most fear of arrest, rather than the people at large. Most people believed that certain groups such as white-collar workers and party members were most vulnerable, and there are many accounts of people resisting promotion in order to stay out of the limelight. Ordinary workers were rarely imprisoned on political charges. Most people seem to have believed Stalin's line that spies and saboteurs were a real danger, and therefore accepted the arrests, including Alexander Solzhenitsyn until his own arrest and later experience of life in the camp system. Other people were still prepared to criticise what they saw as injustices or errors at work, and were not cowed into silence.

Fig. 7 *Beria's relentless pursuit of political deviators filled the slave camps, where they became victims of his thugs. This drawing of one of the camps is by Sergei Korolkoff, once a political prisoner*

Key profile

Alexander Solzhenitsyn

Solzhenitsyn was in the Red Army and captured during the Second World War. After his release, like many other ex-prisoners, he was arrested by the Soviet police and sent to the Gulag. He later wrote about his experiences, became a world famous writer and opponent of the regime, and was eventually allowed to leave the USSR and settle in the USA.

Working conditions

Peasants led hard lives. Conditions in the factories were variable. The industrial workforce more than doubled. Longer-established workers often lived better than new workers, whose standard of living may have declined.

However, workers often supplemented their wages, for example by eating in works canteens. Rationing ended in 1935, and then food prices remained stable whilst wages rose. Despite harsher laws on labour discipline, many workers still found it possible to change jobs. Despite the Stakhanovite propaganda, most targets set for workers were not over-ambitious and were easily met. The Stakhanovite movement actually gave workers more opportunity to demand better conditions and criticise poor management.

■ Cross-reference

For more information on the Stakhanovite movement, see page 57.

■ Activity

Group activity

List any five consequences of the Great Terror in the USSR. Put them in an order of importance, beginning with the most important first. Be prepared to justify your choices and order of choice.

This list can then be the basis for a class discussion on the significance of the terror.

■ Activity

Group activity

Find evidence both to support and contradict each of the following statements in the table below.

Statement	Evidence to support	Evidence to contradict
The Kirov assassination was a key turning point in Stalin's rule.		
The terror had its greatest impact on the Communist Party.		
The terror had a disastrous impact in both town and countryside.		
The most serious impact of the terror was on the armed forces.		
The terror had a greater political impact than an economic impact.		
The USSR was stronger rather than weaker as a result of the terror.		

Learning outcomes

Through your study of this section you should be familiar with the reasons why terror became an increasingly important instrument of State policy in the USSR during the 1930s. You should be able to explain why, although terror had always been part of the regime's policy following the 1917 Revolution and during the Civil War of 1918–21, it became much more significant from the late-1920s onwards, beginning with the war against the peasantry that accompanied collectivisation.

You should be able to explain the importance of events such as Kirov's assassination, and what Stalin's motives were in encouraging and then ending the purges. You should also have some understanding of the debate over the extent to which the purges were carefully manipulated by the State, and the extent to which they were carried forward by their own momentum. You should gain a good understanding of how various individuals and groups of people in the USSR were affected by the purges, and what the immediate and longer-term effects of the terror were on the Soviet economy, political system and society.

In conjunction with other chapters in this book, you should gain some understanding of the debate about the extent to which the use of State coercion, combined with propaganda, was an integral part of what has become known as 'Stalinism'.

AQA Examination-style questions

Read Sources A, B and C and answer the questions that follow.

No area of Soviet life escaped being purged. The constant fear that this created conditioned the whole Soviet people. Under Stalin terror was elevated into a method of government, but the greatest impact of the purges in terms of aggregate numbers was on the middle and lower ranks of Soviet society. Concepts such as innocence and guilt, truth and falsehood, seemed to lose all meaning. The mass of the population were frightened and bewildered. Fear had the effect of destroying moral values and traditional loyalties.

A
*Adapted from M. Lynch, **Stalin and Khrushchev: The USSR 1924–64**, 2001*

By the end of the 1930s a formidable combination of vested interests had become involved in the regime's survival, including full-time Party officials, officials in the central ministries and bureaucrats in the republics, factory directors, the engineers and technical elite, the shop heads and foremen, the Stakhanovites, the better paid and skilled workers, chairmen of collective farms, directors of machine tractor stations, the officer corps, privileged academics, writers, actors and singers. The coming together of these groups contributed a basic source of strength which helped to make totalitarian controls ultimately effective. The terrible purges weakened but did not disrupt the combination. Gaps were rapidly filled by new recruits indebted to the regime.

B
*Adapted from M. Fainsod, **Smolensk Under Soviet Rule**, 1989*

Stalin was aware that the upwardly mobile, once they had acquired their desired position, would become conservative and resistant to change. The tactic adopted to promote change was the permanent purge. The striking factor about the new ruling group was their individual and collective insecurity. The purges affected almost everyone. They made practically everyone two-faced. Officially one agreed with Stalin that life had become better and more cheerful. But in private one returned to the real world, faced with the harsh realities and struggle for existence. However, one had to find the right person to confide in. Everyone became wary of everyone else. The only ones who had little to fear were those on the margin of society. The little man and little woman was much less likely to become a victim.

C
*Adapted from M. McCauley, **Russia 1917–1941**, 1997*

(a) Explain how far the views in Source B differ from
those in Source A in relation to the impact of the
1930s purges on the stability of Soviet society.   *(12 marks)*

Part a) requires the student to compare two sources, and relate the
content to the issue of stability in 1930s USSR. Source A implies that
the purges had a destabilising effect upon Soviet society. Source B
suggests that the terror had a much more limited effect on stability,
because all sorts of people had a 'vested interest' in working together.
The differences in interpretation come about mainly because Source A is
mostly concerned with the impact of terror on the individual. Source B
is making a broader analysis of the impact of terror on society. Therefore
it was possible for individuals to feel frightened and insecure, whilst the
regime itself was strengthened because either people were enthusiastic
about the regime or too frightened to oppose it – which is how many
totalitarian regimes have functioned.

(b) How far did the Great Terror of the 1930s
strengthen the Soviet political and
economic system?   *(24 marks)*

Part b) requires the student to take a broader view of the impact of the
terror. Source C adds to the information already analysed in Sources
A and B. Source C reinforces the message of Source A that in the
atmosphere of a 'permanent purge' people were frightened. However,
Source C also asserts that only the insignificant people, not mentioned
in Source B, were more secure, since they did not have much of a stake in
the system, and therefore did not have much to lose. Source C paints a
contrast between private and public attitudes.

Students are also required to bring their wider knowledge to bear on the
impact of the terror on both the political and economic system, which
is not the same thing as the impact on individuals. There is no simple
answer. It is possible to argue that the political system was strengthened
by the removal of any real opposition to the regime. On the other hand,
it might be argued that it was Stalin's own position rather than the
political health of the country as a whole that was strengthened, and that
political stability could not be advanced in the long run in a society in
which a large section of the population lived in a state of insecurity and
fear. Similarly, it might be argued that the terror, with its great impact on
agriculture and the industrial towns, helped the economy by forcing or
inspiring the population into superhuman efforts.

9 The social impact of Stalin's policies

Activity

Source analysis

What does the speech in Source 1 tell us about the Soviet attitude towards culture?

Key term

Ideological: although 'ideological' can have different shades of meaning, in the context of the USSR it usually refers to the concept that any form of public pronouncement, art, literature, newspapers and so on cannot be divorced from political content. This is because it all has to conform to a Marxist viewpoint as defined by the party. As such, ideology and propaganda become virtually the same thing.

Comrade Stalin has called our writers engineers of human souls. It means knowing life so as to be able to depict it truthfully in works of art, not to depict it in a dead, scholastic way, not simply as 'objective reality' but to depict reality in its revolutionary development… The artistic portayal should be combined with the ideological remoulding and education of the toiling people in the spirit of socialism… This is what we call the method of socialist realism.

 1   *Excerpts from Zhdanov's speech to the founding Congress of the Union of Soviet Writers in 1934*

The role and impact of Stalinist propaganda

Propaganda in NEP Russia

Ever since the 1917 Revolution, the Soviet State had relied extensively upon propaganda to put across important messages. Propaganda depicting both the White opponents of the Bolsheviks and their foreign allies as evil agents of Capitalism, intent on crushing the new revolutionary State, had been an important factor in the Bolsheviks' success in winning the 1917–21 Civil War and consolidating their power. Even during the more peaceful 1920s, the party had used propaganda extensively to justify its policies and get across particular messages. This was important because the population, as discussed on pages 28–32 in particular, was not always receptive to government policies. Propaganda also had a wider **ideological** function: communist enthusiasts did not just want to win support for government policy, but wanted to indoctrinate the population into a different 'Marxist' way of thinking. Art, literature, the cinema, music, architecture, posters and the radio could all be used to mould the 'new' Soviet man, woman and child.

In terms of getting across its message, the Soviet State had a great advantage over democratic societies in which there was less government control of everyday life. The Communists had a monopoly of control over public information, and therefore could prevent any alternative

Fig. 1 *Soviet propaganda poster: 'Compulsory mass literacy campaign', 1930*

view from being presented. Even so, it is difficult to evaluate exactly how effective Soviet propaganda was. Although it was an important part of the Soviet system, the reports collected by party organisations and the security services suggest that there were many ordinary people who were not convinced by the messages put across by the party, particularly when propaganda stridently proclaimed that things were much better than they were in reality.

The Soviet State devoted enormous resources to propaganda, and was quite open about the intention of this. 'Propaganda' was not a term of abuse, something which could be seen as distorting the truth for the benefit of a privileged elite – which was how Communists represented the propaganda spread by the media in the capitalist world. The Soviets were proud of their propaganda efforts, because they were claimed to be a means of spreading the true message to the masses. If the propaganda sometimes seemed crude or over-simplified, that was deliberate. Particularly in the early days of the regime, the Communists believed that the masses of ordinary workers and peasants, who were often poorly educated and 'lacking in political consciousness', would not understand complex messages. Propaganda was just a legitimate extension of education. It was also a means of helping the people on the road to Socialism, and an opportunity to attack the 'enemy'.

The Stalinist approach

Although difficult to prove conclusively, it is likely that propaganda in Stalin's USSR of the 1930s was more effective than the propaganda of the NEP period, because:

■ in the 1920s, communist organisations were relatively new, and certainly not well established in the countryside. Even though the regime tried to influence the peasants to support communist policies, it was competing, often unsuccessfully, with the influence of the Orthodox Church and other village institutions. There were too few committed Communists in the countryside, and many peasants were illiterate. This was to change with collectivisation, since the amalgamation of farms into larger units with a communist-dominated orgainisation gave the regime much more opportunity to influence attitudes and to spread the party line.

■ although Communists did encourage new, revolutionary art forms, much cultural activity in NEP Russia was still relatively free of communist ideology, or was even in competition with it. For example, Western films were more popular with ordinary Russians than the more experimental Soviet cinema of directors like Eisenstein. Soviet films were less about entertainment than strong ideological messages, for example in their depiction of the 1917 Revolution. This was to change in the 1930s as the State progressively took more and more control of all aspects of the media and culture, and tried to influence intellectual life as much as the everyday lives of the masses.

■ A closer look

Eisenstein's *Battleship Potemkin*

Battleship Potemkin, made in 1925, regularly appears in lists of the greatest films ever made. However, it ran for only two weeks when it opened in Moscow. It was far more successful in Berlin, and its propaganda techniques greatly impressed Joseph Goebbels, Hitler's future Minister of Propaganda. The film portrays the mutiny of the crew of the battleship during the 1905 Revolution in Russia. Much of the story has been altered (including the suggestion that there might be a 'happy ending' to the mutiny). The most famous scene in the film, the massacre on the Odessa Steps by the tsar's army, never took place, and was included simply because the director Eisenstein was inspired by the location. The film is full of novel cinematic techniques, and uses ordinary people as well as actors, but is basically a strong propaganda message on behalf of the Communists. It has influenced countless film makers since, not for the politics, but for the techniques.

Although the effectiveness of Soviet propaganda in NEP Russia can be debated, it should be emphasised that when Stalin came to power, there was already much on which to build:

- The regime was already well on the way to reducing illiteracy, which opened up the way for more varieties of propaganda.
- The concept of censorship, for example of the press, was already well established: before the end of 1918, all non-Bolshevik newspapers had been eliminated.
- The regime had done a lot of work in extending the number of schools, and the political content of education, as a means of influencing everyone from the peasant to the party activist.
- Although party organisations such as the Komsomol did not transform all people's attitudes in the 1920s, they were growing in importance, and were undoubtedly having some impact on the new generation of youth. Although not all young people became ardent Communists, there were many who did. These enthusiasts were an important factor in swelling party ranks in the 1930s and helping to drive forward the great projects such as industrialisation, which were as much about propaganda and the ideology of Socialism as about improving people's material lives.

Therefore there had been an important change by 1929. Propaganda and **indoctrination** were already an integral part of the Soviet system, with huge resources devoted to them. The communist regime believed it was right and was acting in the interests of the Soviet people – and therefore had no time for the concept found in liberal Western societies that it was perfectly acceptable, and indeed should be encouraged, for alternative political views or interpretations to be allowed. It was increasingly accepted in the USSR that not only was there just one permissible viewpoint, but no organisation with any independent existence should be tolerated, however well established it was. Hence there were to be increasing conflicts, for example, with the Orthodox Church. Where possible, the regime set up alternative organisations, with a 'politically correct' view, to fill the gap. So, for example, the Komsomol replaced organisations such as the boy scouts. The language of propaganda had become well established by 1929: people were increasingly used to expressions such as 'the enemy', 'the way ahead', 'the need for struggle', and these expressions became even more strident under Stalin in the 1930s. Therefore Stalin already had a strong base from which to spread his own messages.

The role of Stalinist propaganda

Stalin did not drastically alter the organisation of Soviet propaganda in the 1930s. However, there were some distinct developments in the nature and scope of propaganda in this period.

Fig. 2 *Propaganda poster wishing long life to the Komsomols, branches of the Komsomol (Communist Party youth movement)*

Key term

Indoctrination: the process by which governments in particular try to get across certain ideas or policies to their people, usually by extensive use of propaganda techniques.

Stalin's propaganda reached into more corners of the USSR than Soviet propaganda ever had in the 1920s. This was particularly the case in rural areas, where communist influence had often been weak. Collectivisation was the key. Once party activists had helped to organise the peasants into collective or State farms, it was more easy to bombard them with propaganda, because the party had a base in each collective. Peasants were now often forced to attend party meetings. Peasants were also now more likely to be literate, since schools were set up on many collective farms, for adults as well as children, and in the 1930s the government forced teachers to work in places that they would not have chosen of their own free will. Literacy levels were much higher in the 1930s than the 1920s, and the party put across political messages in a variety of ways. It is not likely that many peasants were won over by Soviet propaganda, and police reports testified to this. Many peasants were unimpressed by calls to Socialism or attacks on their churches, and they were more likely to work harder on their small private plots than sweat on the collective for what they were told was 'the good of the Soviet people'. The party may have had more success with its propaganda in the towns and cities, where an increasing number of party members were trained as agitators or organisers of meetings in factories and other places of work. There would be discussions of topical events or public reading of (official) newpapers, always with an ideological slant.

Fig. 3 *Soviet poster: 'The socialist competition transforms work into a matter of honour, glory and heroism' (Stalin), 1931*

Although there had always been government-imposed censorship since the revolution, it became much more rigorous and all-embracing under Stalin. All means of communication were harnessed to the regime's goals of rapid economic and social change, whilst reinforcing the perception of the USSR as surrounded by hostile enemies intent on destroying the emerging socialist society. The possibilities of artistic freedom once available in the 1920s disappeared (page 39). **Socialist Realism**, with its depiction of heroic workers and peasants happily creating an abundant socialist future, was combined with increasingly strident propaganda against the 'enemy', that is, anybody or anything, at home or abroad, that stood in the way of progress as determined by the party. The Stakhanovite movement (page 57) was a prime example of how propaganda was enlisted in the drive for economic progress.

Key term

Socialist Realism: a style of art practised in Stalin's USSR which ensured that all art was propagandist, conveying the message that life under Socialism was happy for ordinary workers and peasants.

The impact of Stalinism on ideology, culture and society

The existence of the Soviet regime relied on a variety of factors:

- The monopoly of power enjoyed by the Communist Party and the impossibility of legally challenging it or replacing it, despite guarantees of civil rights in the Soviet Constitution.
- The threat of force against dissenters or doubters, who were portrayed as being always in the background, and a serious threat to the State and Soviet people. It could be dangerous simply to show insufficient enthusiasm for Stalin's policies, let alone actually oppose them, as seen in the terror.
- The use of propaganda to get support for official policies.
- A natural patriotism, apathy or reluctance of people to oppose the existing government.
- Support that the regime won for its acclaimed successes, for example in the industrialisation drive, and popular admiration for Stalin.

Culture and society in Stalin's USSR

Lenin had been cautious about the possibility of his new regime radically changing Russian culture, at least in the short term. Lenin himself believed that culture transcended class. He admired some aspects of pre-revolutionary culture and was wary of destroying everything from the past, particularly since he felt that Russia was a brutal and brutalised society that did not have enough culture of any sort. Many in the next generation of Communists had fewer scruples than Lenin about starting a cultural revolution. They believed that culture, like the economy and all other aspects of human existence, was based on class, and reflected the interests of the prevailing ruling class. It followed that pre-1917 cultural forms were 'bourgeois' and did not reflect the true feelings or interests of the working class, but had been used instead to reflect and reinforce the dominant interests of the ruling class. Enthusiastic Marxists wanted to create a 'proletarian' culture, or **Proletkult**.

In 1920s NEP Russia, the old and the new sat side by side. Some of the 'new' experimental art forms were not created by committed Communists, but by artists and intellectuals who simply welcomed the initial burst of cultural freedom after 1917. In many cases, they were building on developments that had already begun to flower in late-tsarist Russia. Some were only interested in 'art for art's sake', a Marxist heresy, because it denied the role of culture in helping to shape the 'political consciousness' of the new socialist citizen. This changed under Stalin, when all culture was explicitly linked to propaganda and indoctrination, and there was no such thing as true independent thought. Creativity was encouraged only within defined limits, which were all about what the State decided was good for the party and the people.

The arts in NEP Russia

Lenin had no particular interest in promoting a specific working-class culture. Some experimental artists in the early 1920s accepted the communist message and produced art forms designed to appeal to the masses and also influence them with new ideas, usually portraying a political or ideological message:

- There was a movement for popular theatre, often called **Agitprop** theatre, involving street performances, interaction between audience

Cross-reference

For more on the controls placed on artistic freedom, see pages 118–9. For details of the Stakhanovite movement see page 57.

Activity

Challenge your thinking

As you read this chapter, think about the nature of Soviet propaganda and culture. Was the combination unique to the USSR, or can you see echoes of it in other historical or contemporary periods you may have studied?

and actors, and street processions designed to compete with, and eventually replace, the great religious processions such as Easter.

■ There were radical changes in design and architecture. Constructivists designed everyday objects such as clothes and furniture, incorporating geometric shapes and often influenced by industrial designs. Tatlin and Lissitzky were notable promoters of this art form.

■ Literature encouraged proletarian themes. Mayakovsky was an influential poet who believed that he was writing for the masses, often using radical verse forms.

■ Cinema was taken up enthusiastically by the Communists, who immediately realised its propaganda potential. **Proletkino** made political films. The best known Soviet director was Sergei Eisenstein. His films such as *Battleship Potemkin* and *October* were very political, and also influential outside the USSR because of their brilliant use of new techniques in editing, juxtaposition, the use of music and other techniques far ahead of their time. These efforts later influenced the work of the Nazi propaganda genius Joseph Goebbels in Germany.

A closer look

Some significant representatives of Soviet culture

Stalin was well educated and had a passionate interest in the arts. He had strong views on what he liked and what was good for the USSR – art could not be allowed to flourish without reference to political or social concerns. Some artists rebelled, some conformed, some survived, some were disgraced or worse. The following are some of the best-known cultural figures of the NEP and 1930s periods.

Maxim Gorky (1868–1936)

Already a renowned author in tsarist Russia, Gorky had been enagaged in revolutionary activity, went abroad and returned to Russia after the February Revolution. After a difficult relationship with the Bolsheviks, he lived abroad again between 1921 and 1928, but Stalin persuaded him back because of his reputation. Gorky helped in the development of Socialist Realism, but relationships with the party were never smooth. Gorky died whilst undergoing medical treatment. Was he murdered on Stalin's orders?

Sergei Eisenstein (1898–1948)

A Latvian who fought with the Red Army in the Civil War, Eisenstein built up the Soviet film industry with a string of brilliant semi-historical epic silent films, notably *Battleship Potemkin* (1925) and *October* (1928). He fell out of favour in the cultural revolution, and worked abroad, but returned in 1938 with a public confession of his errors. He made the patriotic epic *Alexander Nevsky*, with a strong anti-German message. His final epic, about the despotic Tsar *Ivan the Terrible*, drew uncomfortable parallels with Stalin, and was not shown until after Stalin's death.

Vladimir Mayakovsky (1893–1930)

Mayakovsky was a futurist poet and dramatist, whose most famous work was probably his epic poem about Lenin, written after Lenin's death. Mayakovsky was a revolutionary artist but not a party member, and his later works attacked bureaucracy. He fell out of favour and committed suicide. He was later regarded as an early

Fig. 4 *Joseph Stalin with Maxim Gorky*

practitioner of Socialist Realism. But had he lived longer, would he have survived Stalin's purges?

Mikhail Sholokhov (1905–84)

Sholokhov wrote highly praised and successful novels in the 1930s – notably *Quiet Flows The Don* and *Virgin Soil Upturned*. His themes were Cossack life and collectivisation. He became very wealthy, partly because he kept the party line. Although Sholokhov criticised the treatment of the kulaks, Stalin, who loved good literature, protected him.

Kasimir Malevich (1878–1955), Vladimir Tatlin (1885–1955), Lazar Lissitzky (1890–1941)

These were some of the futurist artists and designers who took advantage of the new freedoms after 1917 to experiment with subjects ranging from great monuments to household objects like chairs.

Dmitri Shostakovich (1906–75)

One of Russia's greatest modern composers, Shostakovich was very successful in the 1920s and 1930s until Stalin criticised his opera *Lady Macbeth* for what he regarded as its incomprehensibility. Shostakovich never wrote another opera, although he confessed his errors and his 1937 Fifth Symphony was known as *A Soviet Artist's Reply to Just Criticism*.

Culture in Stalin's USSR: cultural revolution 1928–31

1928, the year of the First Five Year Plan and collectivisation, saw an accompanying cultural revolution that lasted for about three years. It was a combination of two themes: a class war that attacked old values, associated with the NEP; and a projection of the new society that was to emerge out of the great economic revolution taking place in the towns and countryside. Reservations, such as Lenin had expressed, about a gradualist approach to cultural development were swept aside. There was to be no compromise, and only a 'proletarian' approach was acceptable. It led to new and sometimes more violent attacks on religion and old art forms. There was a strong sense of what was called **Utopianism**, planning for the ideal proletarian future. This was reflected in the planning of modern cities, which were to include huge palaces for the people, such as a monumental Palace of the Soviets that was planned for, but never built, on the site of a cathedral in Moscow. The once-praised film director Eisenstein was now criticised for making films that did not emphasise enough the important role of ordinary workers and peasants in Soviet society. Films, books and theatre had to have straightforward, optimistic, easily understood messages that made heroes out of ordinary people and showed the building of a new and better society. Guidelines were issued to writers and artists. Plots had to have a happy ending – at least for true Communists. This was Socialist Realism, which used the arts to depict the Soviet Utopian vision of society, not the reality. So, for example, paintings of villages showed an abundance of corn and contented peasants, even if the reality was class warfare and devastating famine in the countryside. Music was also expected to be optimistic and jolly. The works of some of the greatest living composers such as Shostakovich were criticised personally by Stalin for being incomprehensible to the masses, and some works were banned.

> **Key term**
>
> **Utopianism:** a belief in a future idealised society.

Fig. 5 *Joseph Stalin, painting by F. Schurpin*

A good way to support your study of NEP and Stalinist Russia would be to explore some of the arts from Soviet Russia that have stood the test of time.

Two good reads are:

1 the novel *We* by Evgeny Zamyatin (1920). This book was never officially published in the USSR, because it is a satire on the new communist system. It describes a totally regulated world of the future where all workers live in identical conditions and there is no individuality because everything is subordinated to the needs of the State. Although not known much in the West, *We* was a considerable influence on George Orwell, as can be seen in his better known book *1984*.

2 Anatoli Rybakov's novel *Children of the Arbat*. This novel was suppressed in the USSR for many years. It tells the story of Russians who suffered in the purges, intertwined with a fascinating psychological portrait of Stalin, as he plots the assassination of Kirov and prepares to unleash a reign of terror.

If you are interested in music, sample the works of Shostakovich: for example his *Leningrad Symphony*, so-called because it was written during the Siege of Leningrad which began in 1941.

Eisenstein's classic films are worth seeing for their propaganda techniques: especially *Battleship Potemkin* and *October*, a 1920s interpretation of the original 1917 Revolution.

Nothing was left to chance. In 1931, the existing Artist Association in the USSR became the Association of Proletarian Artists, and only those who promoted Socialist Realism could practise their craft. Other artists, whatever their artistic merit, were excluded. Similarly in literature **RAPP** (The Russian Association of Proletarian Writers) controlled the output of authors to ensure that Socialist Realism prevailed, with themes relating to party concerns such as industrialisation, with titles such as *How The Steel Was Tempered*. Artists conformed, were silenced by the State, or remained silent of their own accord, such as the novelist Boris Pasternak. One of Russia's greatest living writers, Maxim Gorky, toed the party line, declaring that, under Stalin, Russian writers had 'lost nothing but the right to be bad writers'. Writers were expected to dirty their hands and work on industrial and agricultural sites. Cheap books were produced in bulk to ensure that an increasingly literate population lapped up the propaganda.

In 1931, however, Stalin declared that the cultural revolution had come to an end. The intelligentsia acquired a new status. Provided they toed the official line, they were treated very well, and became very successful and wealthy. In contrast, those who did not conform suffered badly. Many hundreds of intellectuals and artists disappeared during the Great Terror, many of them executed. In April 1932, all existing proletarian artistic organisations were merged into one single union, and Stalin's hold over cultural life was complete.

Education

There was a similar shift in policy towards education. After the revolution there had been a period of experimentation with an interest in progressive techiques. These involved more active learning, and a less authoritarian method of teaching as in the past. However, although there were increased numbers of children attending school, the system ran into major difficulties for both ideological and practical reasons. Teachers in the 1920s were often untrained and had little authority, having to share responsibilities with committees and being forbidden to exercise discipline. Most teachers were not Communists and did not understand nor approve of the new methods. Some Communists wanted to do away with schools altogether. There were insufficient resources for schools, and in some areas the numbers attending schools actually began to fall. During the cultural revolution the acquisition of knowledge was despised and there was an emphasis on school children doing socially useful work outside the school. Traditional teachers were driven out and replaced by more committed Communists. Students from a proletarian background were given priority on higher education courses, although these were often of poor quality and there was a very high drop-out rate. Examinations were scrapped.

Stalin saw the results of experimentation as disastrous. The USSR needed a more educated and skilled workforce, and experiments were failing. The need for skilled workers, scientists and technicians led to the reintroduction of more organised school structures and traditional methods, even to the extent of reintroducing school uniforms. More emphasis was put on higher training of specialists who could help the industrialisation drive, with courses in mathematics, science and technology.

There was very centralised control over education, provided by **Narkompros**, the People's Commissariat for Enlightenment. Education started at the nursery at 3 years, then infant school or kindergarten until 7, then secondary school to at least 15. Parents were expected to contribute towards the cost of secondary schooling. There were also many adult education institutions. Practical needs triumphed over ideology, although a particular political slant was still put on subjects like history, which was presented very much from a Marxist viewpoint, especially when it concerned Russian history. There was also considerable emphasis on learning the importance of duty and loyalty. Teachers were now of higher status, and were more likely to be party members. Eighty per cent of university students were ethnic Russians, Ukrainians or Jews.

The social impact of Stalinism

The upheavals caused by Stalin's economic revolution from the late-1920s onwards inevitably had an impact on Soviet society at all levels. The impact varied between particular groups.

Women in NEP Russia

Soviet policy towards the role and status of women had always been inconsistent. The Bolsheviks had maintained a belief in gender equality, and soon after the revolution women were awarded equal rights and opportunities to men, provided they belonged to the 'right' social class. However, the reality was that leading members of the party showed little real interest in the realities of women's lives, reflecting the fact that Russian society had been traditionally male dominated. When the party reluctantly agreed to set up women's sections in the party, the intention was that the women party members should explain party policy to other women, rather than create party policy. By the time of Lenin's death in 1924, the party had created women's sections in most provinces. However, the leader of the All-Russian Women's Department had failed to turn the organisation into an effective pressure group. **Zhenotdel**, the Women's Section of the Central Committee, created with the aim of encouraging more women to play a prominent part in public life, was not popular and was closed down in 1930. More women did get involved in local Soviets and other party organisations and activities, but they generally met with a lack of enthusiasm or outright prejudice,

Fig. 6 *Propaganda poster by A. Radakov: 'The illiterate is like a blind man', 1920*

Key term

Narkompros: the party organisation responsible for education.

particularly in rural areas where traditional attitudes still held sway, but also within the party itself. For example, it was seen as inappropriate for women to take an active part in politics, even if they were married to party members. Male Communists still expected their wives to stay at home and look after them. The family was still important. Although some Communists experimented with communes and radical ideas like abolishing any form of commitment between individuals in favour of free love, such departures from the norm were relatively rare – Russian society was still conservative in many respects.

Equality in law had limited impact in practice. When unemployment rose in NEP Russia, women tended to be pushed into lower paid unskilled work, often in domestic work. The number of unemployed women steadily rose during the 1920s. The proportion of women in factory work in 1929 was very similar to before the First World War, although this was soon to change significantly during the 1930s. There was also social inequality. For example, men had to give very little notice to divorce their wives, and then took no further responsibility for their welfare. Because men who deserted their wives or girlfriends had no legal repsonsibility for them, all men were required to pay a special tax to meet the needs of single mothers. Simplified divorce procedures in 1926 (one partner simply had to fill out a form) led to rocketing divorce rates, and almost half of women who did divorce were unemployed or economically dependent on their husbands. Therefore for these women, there was little meaningful 'freedom'.

Soviet propaganda painted a very different picture to reality. In NEP Russia, many women were criticised for preferring Hollywood films or 'decadent' activities like dancing to solid working-class virtues. The ideal Soviet woman, as was to be increasingly portrayed in Stalinist propaganda, was supposed to be proudly independent and to reject outdated bourgeois concepts such as worrying about make-up and displaying their femininity. Loyalty to the party and State was promoted above the ideals of romantic love or loyalty to a husband or family, as in this Soviet poem (Source 2):

Fig. 7 *Propaganda poster marking the 1930 International March of Women Workers and illustrating woman working in a textile factory*

> Save your yelling mama
>
> No need to give me dark looks
>
> I'm going to sign up for Komsomol
>
> And I'm going to read some books
>
> I don't have use for rings now
>
> And bracelets not at all
>
> Because together with my girlfriend
>
> I've got my eyes set on a guy
>
> From the Komsomol.

2   *Traditional Soviet poem*

Women in the party

By 1928, only about 65,000 out of 1 million party members were women. Female membership of the Komsomol never rose above 20 per cent in the towns and 5 per cent in the countryside. The percentage of women in the party actually fell during the 1920s. It was reported in the Moscow region that the wives of party members opposed the entry of new female members into the party on the grounds that they only wanted to seduce their husbands. The party discriminated as much as society at large. Women party members scarcely enjoyed the same benefits as men. One of the few prominent female party members was Alexandra Kollontai (1872–1952). Alexandra was a member of the Central Committee and Commissar for Social Welfare after the 1917 Revolution. However, she soon had policy disagreements with Lenin and was demoted to less significant posts, and her radical ideas on the role of women in communist society were not adopted, although she was responsible for some social legislation. When local party organisations were told to purge members for being 'passive' (that is, inactive) members, women were more likely than men to be expelled. The few well-educated female party members who did rise to positions with some authority often found themselves harrassed or ignored. Not surprisingly, many women simply did not believe party propaganda about the joys of equality and freedom.

Fig. 8 *Left: 1928 drawing of fashionable women in NEP Russia. Right: The reality of life for most Soviet women in 1928. (Courtesy of John Laver)*

Soviet women and the family in the 1930s

Under Stalin there was no significant improvement in women's status or conditions. The disruption caused by collectivisation and industrialisation had a particularly negative impact. Rapid urbanisation caused severe housing problems, especially overcrowding. In such conditions, increasing numbers of men deserted their wives or girlfriends, especially after the birth of children. A high proportion of the millions of women who joined the workforce for the first time were in low paid jobs or were the sole breadwinner for their family.

Women who remained married were classified as 'enemies of the people' if their husbands became victims of the purges. During the period of the Five Year Plans, women factory workers do not appear to have been noticeably more enthusiastic about their work than peasant women. Women workers were usually paid less than male workers, who were likely to be more skilled. Women were more likely than men to become unemployed, and not get compensation. Women in this position often appeared on the fringes of society: for example, numbers of prostitutes in cities rose. The failure of women to get injustices overturned in the courts led to several strikes and protests, and a further unwillingness on the part of all but the most committed to give up time for activities such as attending party-organised meetings in the workplace.

The State did eventually recognise that there was a problem. In the early days of the regime, ardent Communists had criticised the family as an outdated bourgeois concept. A law in 1920 meant that Russia became the first European country to legalise abortion on demand, in an attempt to give women freedom of choice. Russia soon had the highest divorce rate in Europe (although also the highest marriage rate!), even though housing shortages often compelled divorced couples to continue living together. However, the regime in the 1930s suddenly became positively pro-family, as part of what became known as the '**Great Retreat**'. This was a conscious rejection of the social experiments of the post-revolutionary period. It was strongly influenced by the evidence of falling birth rates and and the disruption caused by family break-ups. The regime was particularly alarmed by reports of large numbers of orphaned and abandoned children and a soaring juvenile crime rate. There were several million orphans in the USSR throughout this period. The NKVD became involved in trying to get some of these homeless children into State-run institutions, and parents were held legally responsible for their children's behaviour. The decline of family life was now seen as a great social evil. Action was taken in the Family Code of May 1936:

- Abortion was made illegal, and this did have the impact of increasing the birth rate in the late-1930s.

- It was made more difficult to obtain a divorce. It was made more costly and both parties had to attend the proceedings.

- Mothers with six or more children received cash payments.

- Propaganda now focused on the irresponsibility of husbands and fathers who neglected their responsibilities. Child support payments were fixed, although they were difficult to collect, since many men married several times.

- At a similar time (April 1935) the law was tightened so that children who committed violent crimes were treated like adults from the age of 12 upwards.

- New laws were passed against prostitution and homosexuality (although the USSR regarded these as 'capitalist vices' and was reluctant to accept their existence).

There was a wives' movement to try to improve the status of women, but it was run by women from the elite and was mostly concerned with emphasising the need for women to show duty towards their husbands and families. None of this

Fig. 9 *1926 Soviet cartoon satirising Soviet bureaucracy. (Courtesy of John Laver)*

significantly improved women's lives – although working-class women may have preferred the new laws after the chaos of the NEP years, which in practice had clearly favoured men. One new benefit to women was in higher education: 60 per cent of undergraduates were women by 1940. However, poorer women, as in the past, were expected to look after their children and homes even though they now had the additional burden of contributing much more to the full-time workforce as part of the drive to construct Socialism. Women struggled with a situation in which there were insufficient kindergartens for the children of working women. The already small proportion of educated women in party or high administrative posts declined even further in the 1930s compared to the 1920s. Women in the Asian Islamic republics had even lower status. As part of the regime's commitment to equal rights Stalin wrote in 1937:

> The triumph of socialism has filled women with enthusiasm and mobilised the women of our Soviet land to become active in culture, to master machinery, to develop a knowledge of science and to be active in the struggle for high labour productivity.

If Stalin really believed this, he did not know his own country. He asserted that there was no need for a strategy to promote female emancipation, since women would automatically be liberated by the coming of Socialism. In the meantime, women were to be regarded as an economic resource that should be directed at fulfilling the Five Year Plans.

Living standards in the 1930s

The impact of Stalin's economic policies has already been described in Chapters 4 and 6. To summarise the overall living conditions for most Soviet citizens, this period can be subdivided as follows:

- Everyday life was hard from 1929 to about 1935. During this period there was rationing. The Great Famine of 1932–3 not only caused millions of deaths, but caused major problems in towns as they were swamped with refugees from the countryside and the rationing system often broke down. Internal passports were introduced in 1932, along with urban registration. City dwellers needed residence permits and illegal residents, if caught, were expelled. There was an acute housing shortage, even though housing space was allocated by local authorities. Many families were crammed into communal apartments, whilst many workers lived in barracks at their factories. Many cities were without sewage, street lighting and public transport, despite show projects such as the Moscow metro. Water was rationed. There was considerable 'hooliganism' or urban violence. Many people depended on the black market for survival. Living standards dropped considerably, with 1933 being the worst year: popular consumption was lower than in 1900, and consumption of meat was only a third of the 1928 figure.

- Conditions improved from 1935, with 1937 being probably the best year for living standards. Because of major shortages (acquiring shoes was a particular problem), some private trades such as shoe-repair, hairdressing and plumbing were made legal again.

Fig. 10 *1925 drawing: Alcoholism was a persistent problem in the USSR. (Courtesy of John Laver)*

■ **Activity**

Revision exercise

1 For each of the following headings, make a comparison that lists any similarities and differences between the situation in the mid-1920s and the mid-1930s:

- ■ Family
- ■ Women
- ■ Education
- ■ Living conditions
- ■ Working conditions

2 Is it possible to say what Stalin's Russia meant for a 'typical' family?

3 Were Russians better off in 1941 than in 1924?

Fig. 11 *The cover of a satirical Soviet magazine showing a well-fed priest and hungry peasant side-by-side. (Courtesy of John Laver)*

■ Problems increased again after 1937. The impact of a bad harvest in 1936 was felt, and living standards for many people dropped again. There was a continued rise in the urban population, putting further strain on public services.

■ Urban workers often coped better with shortages than peasants. Some factory workers benefited from their workplaces providing canteens and even shops, filled with produce bought from the countryside for the employees to purchase.

When war came in 1941, conditions for civilians as well as soldiers became very harsh, and rationing was re-introduced.

Religion

Religion as a concept was rejected by Communists. As Marxists, they believed that religious observance distracted people from the vital task of developing their social and class awareness and, under the leadership of the Communist Party, working for a socialist transformation of society. Communists regarded the Russian Orthodox Church, which had been an important ally of the tsarist regime, as a tool of class repression exercised by bourgeois rulers against ordinary people. However, the Soviet State as developed by Lenin was not an atheist State: it confiscated Church property; issued hostile propaganda against it; persecuted its priests; and promoted a materialist rather than spiritualist interpretation of the world. But it did not actually ban religion. There was a practical reason for this. The Orthodox Church commanded the loyalty of many millions of Russians, especially in rural areas. There was a split between traditionalists within the Church and the 'Living Church', which was made up of reformers. However, although the party tried to widen this rift, it had limited impact. Other religions, notably Islam in some of the Asian republics, also had a strong hold on the population.

Therefore in NEP Russia the State focused mainly on propaganda and education to spread the message about the false promises of hope and salvation spread by religion. Anti-religious publications spread the message, and activists sometimes campaigned against individual priests. Members of the Komsomol often destroyed religious icons, removed sacred relics from churches, disrupted festivals like Easter and even created rival festivals. Sometimes activities backfired, as when the party organised public debates with Church representatives. The resulting publicity did more for the Church than the party, and there were many peasant complaints about anti-religious activity. Traditionalists benefited from the backlash against persecution, and there is evidence of increasing resistance to change and a religious revival. In some areas, such as the Ukraine, the party actually stopped anti-religious campaigns because it was realised that they were counter-productive.

Under Stalin, the regime lost patience once it was realised that people could not be persuaded to renounce their religious beliefs. In 1929, the regime resorted to a much more direct attack:

■ The teaching of religious creeds was banned.

■ Hundreds of churches were destroyed or shut down (many were re-opened in the Second World War so that the population could pray for a Soviet victory!)

■ All religious schools were closed.

Although there was a brief relaxation of the campaign against religion in 1935, it was soon renewed with vigour, and many priests had to function in secret.

Despite the dangers of expressing controversial opinions, in the 1937 census over half a million Soviet citizens described themselves as religious believers. The number of believers was actually much higher and, for all its efforts, the regime found it impossible to kill off religious belief, and not just in the Orthodox Church. Jewish schools and synagogues were closed. Islamic practices, very widespread in the Asian republics, such as fasting and wearing of the veil, were banned or discouraged. However, many Soviet citizens held on to their faith.

Ideology and opinion in Stalin's USSR

Although it is tempting to assume that in a dictatorship or totalitarian society such as the USSR there was no such thing as public opinion, since the State controlled all major means of communication, it cannot be assumed that all people held the same views. Nevertheless, it is not easy to gauge public opinion in a 'closed' society such as Stalin's USSR, in which citizens were positively discouraged from expressing their true feelings and there were no permitted channels through which to publish views that departed from the 'official' line. This was particularly true during the dangerous years of the terror. However, it is also true that the regime was very keen to know what people *were* thinking. Therefore the security police spent much of its time compiling reports on public opinion. These reports were then summarised, and the summaries were sent upwards to the top leaders. In addition, ordinary citizens sent millions of letters to political leaders and institutions on a range of subjects such as abuse of authority by local bureaucrats. This was a tradition that had continued from tsarist times. Also, although there was only one candidate in each local election, there were often lively pre-election meetings to decide who that candidate should be, and strong opinions might be expressed at these meetings. Major institutions such as the party, its youth wing the Komsomol, and the Army's political administration all reported on public opinion.

The regime, including Stalin himself, certainly learned a lot from these reports. The leaders knew that the regime, or aspects of it, was not very popular amongst many people and in many areas. They knew of specific attitudes, such as rising anti-Semitism in some areas, or hostility to rising prices. The regime was aware that people often expressed their frustrations in jokes, often with a strong political content, such as 'When we catch the capitalist countries (a favourite theme of Soviet propaganda), can we stay there?' It is difficult to judge whether these reports ever had much influence on official policy. Although there were negative sentiments expressed, this does not mean that the regime was on shaky ground. Stalin's regime could count on a certain amount of good will, generated by several factors:

- The regime did associate itself with the idea of progress and modernisation – which had a positive impact on many young people.
- Soviet propaganda may have had some success in portraying the regime as the guardian of national security and patriotism, and therefore something that should be supported even if there might be grumblings against specific problems such as shortages. Stalin was to cleverly use this sentiment in the Second World War, by calling on the people to fight for Mother Russia rather than for Communism.
- Conditions did improve at times in the 1930s, and people understood that the State did provide for some basic needs such as housing, food and education, even when they were not of sufficient quality or quantity.

Activity
Research exercise

1. Research the different religions practised in the USSR (remember that there were different variants of Christianity as well as non-Christian religions).

2. For the various religions you have examined consider the extent to which their position had been strengthened or weakened as the result of developments since 1924.

   You may like to give a class presentation on what you have found out.

Fig. 12 *Propaganda poster by Alexandre Samokjvalov: 'On the occasion of the 7th anniversary of the revolution, long live the communist youth organisation. Young people are going to take over', 1924*

Stalin himself was usually immune from criticism – people often blamed problems on other local officials and assumed that Stalin did not know about them. The image of Stalin as a firm but caring father-figure was very strong in Soviet propaganda.

There was simply no easy nor safe means by which people could express a desire for radical change, and the State's monopoly control of the media gave younger people in particular little opportunity to consider alternative paths.

Activity

Consider these statements:

- Stalin's regime rested more on popular consent than on force for its stability and continued existence.
- Religion posed the biggest internal threat to the communist regime.
- The popularity of religion declined in the USSR between 1924 and 1941.
- Marxist/communist ideology underpinned all popular culture in the USSR.
- Soviet people were better educated in 1941 than in 1924.
- There was no personal freedom in the USSR.
- Women had more equality by 1941 compared to 1924.
- The family was a less stable unit by 1941.
- There was no great literature or music in Stalin's USSR.
- The cinema was the most important means of spreading Soviet propaganda.
- Town dwellers were better off than those living in the countryside.
- Living standards rose in the 1930s.
- The Stalinist regime could not have survived without censorship.
- Socialist Realism was incompatible with great art.
- Communist ideology had a great attraction for Soviet youth.

1. Decide which of the above statements are facts and which are opinions. How many of these statements are true?

2. Is it possible to judge what the impact of Stalinist or communist ideology was on ordinary people or on the USSR as a whole?

Activity

Challenge your thinking

How important was ideology to the success of Stalin's regime?

Summary questions

1. Explain why there was a cultural revolution under Stalin.

2. How far were the lives of ordinary Soviet citizens changed by Stalin?

3. How far did Stalin's regime rest on consent, and to what extent on force?

10   What was Stalinism?

In this chapter you will learn about:

- the nature of Stalinism and how it developed to 1941
- the role of key institutions and organisations such as the Communist Party
- how Stalinism affected people's lives
- the strengths and weaknesses of the USSR on the eve of war in 1941.

Fig. 1 *Propaganda poster entitled: 'We will achieve abundance', 1949*

Stalin ordered a postage stamp to be printed with his image. However, complaints soon got back that the stamps would not stick to envelopes. Stalin ordered an investigation. The secret police reported back.

'Comrade Stalin,' a commissar said hesitantly, 'The stamps are in excellent condition and the glue is of the highest quality. The problem is that people are spitting on the wrong side.'

1

A Soviet joke from the 1930s

■ The strengths and weaknesses of the USSR on the eve of war in 1941

The German invasion of the USSR in June 1941 was a catastrophic event for the Soviet people. Although they emerged victorious in 1945, it was at an enormous price in terms of loss of life, material damage and psychological hurt. Stalin, after early costly mistakes, emerged as an effective war leader, and his leadership was just one factor in the Soviet victory. It is almost certain that the USSR would not have survived the war had Stalin's industrialisation programme not been carried out. This was because for all the heroism and sacrifice of Soviet soldiers and civilians during the war, it was the ability of the State to mobilise great depths of industrial muscle that eventually led to Germany's defeat, once the Soviets had managed to survive the initial German onslaught in 1941.

Strengths

- The USSR survived the war against Germany that began in June 1941, suggesting that the USSR must have had considerable strengths given the formidable nature of the German war machine.
- Stalin's industrialisation programme had given the USSR a strong industrial base enabling it to compete with other Powers, including when at war. For example, the USSR was able to build on this base after 1941 to significantly outproduce Germany in war materials and heavy industry, despite the devastation caused by the German invasion.
- The centralised nature of the Stalinist command economy enabled it to adapt relatively quickly to the needs of total war. Total war means a situation in which the government organised the whole of society and the economy to meet the needs of the war effort.
- Stalinist propaganda during the 1930s had already created a 'siege mentality' amongst the Soviet people. The people were used to hardship and exhortations to greater effort, and adapted to the crisis of war.
- Stalin was respected as a strong leader.
- For all their faults, the Five Year Plans had achieved remarkable growth, and gave the USSR a strong base for further development. Achievements included some of the great hydro-electric projects and an increase in steel production by 400 per cent and in coal production by almost 600 per cent between 1928 and 1941. Some republics such as Georgia saw significant economic development for the first time.
- Although consumer goods were not a priority, availability improved as the Five Year Plans developed.
- Education became much more widespread, with a considerable increase in literacy.
- The workforce gradually became more skilled.
- There was a development in basic social services such as health.
- Living standards were probably beginning to rise again after a considerable fall in the early 1930s.
- More facilities such as schools became available in rural areas, although they still lagged behind the towns.
- Stalin's regime did inspire enthusiasm amongst some ardent Communists, particularly younger ones.
- There was a certain amount of social mobility, and it was possible for people to 'rise through the ranks'.

Fig. 2 *Moscow, 7 November 1941. After their parade on the 'Red Square', the Red Army troops are directly sent to the front*

Weaknesses

■ Stalin's economic policies caused immense disruption to many people's lives, both in urban and rural areas.

■ Terror was an integral part of Stalin's policies, and millions of people were killed, imprisoned or suffered in other ways. Family life was disrupted. Many people lived in fear.

■ Economic policies had limited success. Agriculture remained a weakness, with low yields and an unenthusiastic workforce.

■ The urban workforce lived hard lives, with strict labour discipline and harsh conditions.

■ There were many social problems caused, for example, by poor and overcrowded housing, and deficiencies in public services.

■ Most women remained second-class citizens in several respects.

■ There was no personal or political freedom. Religious believers were often persecuted. There was no free press. All cultural activity was controlled by the State. People could not travel freely. There were no free elections.

■ The population was bombarded with constant propaganda.

The nationalities

In addition, Stalin's rule had proved a very difficult period for the various nationalities who made up the USSR. In 1939, almost 100 million out of 170 million Soviet citizens were not Russian, and a further 20 million non-Russians were annexed to the USSR in 1939–40 when it absorbed eastern Poland and the Baltic States. The largest groups amongst the non-Russians were Ukrainians at 28 million (although they were fellow Slavs, the same racial group as Russians) and just over 5 million Belorussians (also Slavs). Other sizeable groups

Activity

Group activity

1 Draw up your own balance sheet of strengths and weaknesses of the USSR in 1941. Pick five strengths and five weaknesses from the lists on these pages, or any others you can think of, and rank your strengths and weaknesses in order of importance.

2 Compare your lists with those of other students, and work out which are the most common choices. This can form the basis of a class discussion, or a 'class essay' on the condition of the USSR in 1941, to which all students contribute a part.

were Kazakhs (3 million), Uzbeks (almost 5 million), Tatars (over 4 million), Jews (3 million), Georgians, Azeri and Armenians (over 2 million each). The Union of Soviet Socialist Republics, consolidated in the 1924 Constitution, was already well established by the time Stalin came to power. The USSR was a federation, meaning a union of equal States or republics, and the constitution allowed any State to leave the federation if it so wished. The reality was different: the USSR was a centralised State, with control exercised from Moscow by the Communist Party. The party recruited members of national minorities to government and party posts within their own republics, and local culture was encouraged to some extent. Education was made compulsory throughout the USSR.

The economic revolution had a major impact on the republics. Collectivisation had a devastating effect on some economies, for example Kazakhstan, whilst Uzbekistan's agriculture was decimated in order to produce cotton to supply Russian industry. Some of the great industrial projects were sited outside Russia, for example the Dnieper Dam in the Ukraine and the Turksib Railway linking Siberia with Central Asia. But the Ukraine suffered terribly from famine during collectivisation.

Once the economic revolution met resistance after 1929, Stalin adopted a much more ruthless policy of centralisation and promoting ethnic Russians. There was some urbanisation in the republics, but the new towns were often dominated by ethnic Russian, Polish, Jewish or Armenian migrants. Although nationalities were educated in their own languages, Russian was also made compulsory in 1938, and Russian was the 'official' language, for example in the Soviet army. The nationalities also suffered in the terror, with a wave of national deportations beginning in the late-1930s. In 1937, a large Korean minority was deported from the Far Eastern region to Central Asia when war with Japan was threatened. Poles and Germans were deported from near the Western frontiers in the late-1930s. Extensive purges were carried out in the newly annexed parts of Poland and the Baltic States in 1939 and 1940. In 1941, over 400,000 Volga Germans were deported to Siberia and Central Asia. Whilst there is no evidence of mass nationalist discontent at this time, life for Soviet citizens outside Russia itself was just as difficult in the 1930s as for most Russians. The anti-religious campaign spread into Ukraine and Belorussia. There was direct persecution of Islam in the Central Asian republics after 1928. Mosques were closed and many Islamic practices attacked. A campaign against the veiling of women had already begun in 1927. Pilgrimages abroad to Mecca, which were the highlight of Muslims' lives, were made illegal in 1935. There were sporadic revolts against 'Sovietisation' but they were not effective. Islamic beliefs were not destroyed, just as Christianity survived in Russia. Those 'national Communists' within the republics who

Fig. 3 *Propaganda poster celebrating the efforts of the men and women of numerous races that made up the Soviet Union, 1934*

showed distaste for centralising policies were purged, and virtually the entire party leaderships of the non-Russian republics were replaced in 1937–8 by colleagues more compliant with Moscow. Although Stalin's regime was secure, the foundations for the nationalist discontent that flowered in the years just before the break-up of the USSR in 1991 had already been laid in Stalin's time.

What was Stalinism and its overall impact on the USSR in this period?

'Stalinism' was not an expression used by Stalin himself or by anyone else during the 1930s. It came into wide use only after Stalin's death in 1953 to identify the main political, economic and social characteristics of the USSR as it developed under Stalin's leadership. These characteristics were modified after 1953, but remained the fundamental basis of the Soviet State until its break-up in 1991. There have been many attempts to define Stalinism. One useful one was suggested by Graeme Gill in *Stalinism* (1990). He identified six key features:

1 Personal dictatorship.

2 A 'command economy' that was centrally controlled and directed.

3 A politicisation of life, meaning that all human activity was given a political slant. This was determined by the State or the party. Citizens did not have the the freedom to behave as individuals, but were expected to conform to what was considered the norm. The good of the community was more important than the rights of the individual.

4 A social structure that in theory allowed for equality of all people and enabled anyone to rise to a position of influence through ability or commitment. However, in practice, the Communist Party dominated all aspects of life; its members were marked out from other people, and those with senior positions in the party had most privileges.

5 A culture whose content was determined by the State. It did not allow creative energy to blossom, but rather subordinated all cultural and intellectual activity to suit the ideology of the ruling regime.

6 A conservative ethos. This meant that the party hierachy, whilst preaching a revolutionary creed based on Marxist–Leninist philosophy, in practice became conservative and in many respects was resistant to change.

Stalin's dictatorship

Stalin's USSR from 1936 described itself as a socialist society in which the State and the party represented the interests of the workers and peasants. Society was organised in their interests rather than the interests of one dominant group. It was the dictatorship of the proletariat rather than the dictatorship of a political party or individual. The reality was very different. The USSR was always a dictatorship of the Communist Party. Under Stalin, it effectively became a personal dictatorship because, although the party dominated the population, Stalin himself increasingly dominated the party. There was no official position of 'leader'. But as General Secretary of the party, Stalin was unchallenged after 1929.

This does not mean that the USSR was a completely totalitarian society subject to every whim of a dictator, although it has sometimes been

Fig. 4 *Propaganda poster showing a much-loved Stalin with a montage of adoring supporters, c.1940–5*

Fig. 5 *Joseph Stalin (1879–1953), Soviet statesman with children, Moscow, 1936*

interpreted in that way. A totalitarian society is one in which the State controls every aspect of people's lives, not just physically, but even their thoughts and opinions. The USSR came close to being this through a mixture of propaganda, education and force, but it was never completely totalitarian. This was partly because it was not efficient enough, and partly because there were always some people who were not brainwashed into accepting the official line – whether they were religious believers, peasants resisting collectivisation, workers who did not respond enthusiastically to calls to increase production, or others. There were individuals who might conform outwardly, but kept their own thoughts private. There were a minority of people who actively tried to resist the regime, unsuccessfully.

Stalin had most of the attributes of a dictator. He allowed a massive cult of personality to grow around him. He was increasingly represented in Soviet propaganda as almost a God-like figure, the wise, all-knowing father and protector of his people, the true successor of Lenin and guardian of the revolution. Privately, Stalin sometimes cricitised the excesses of this personality cult – for example he refused a request to rename Moscow as Stalinodar – but he generally went along with the cult or perhaps encouraged it.

Many of Stalin's actions, particularly during the Great Terror, can be interpreted as an attempt to strengthen his control over the party and thereby the USSR as a whole. This may have been due to paranoia – a fear of being opposed or replaced; it may have been personal ambition; it may have been a genuine belief that he was the best man to take the country forward. Probably it was a combination of several factors.

As one historian wrote:

> The Soviet Union was a totalitarian state, but this did not mean that it was characterised by perfect central control. Far from it. The more Stalin concentrated in his own hands power over specific areas of politics, the greater the lack of compliance he encountered in others. His USSR was a mixture of exceptional orderliness and exceptional disorderliness. So long as the chief official aims were to build up military and heavy-industrial strength the reality of the situation was disguised from him... Stalin had only the dimmest awareness of the problems he had created... His policies were a mixture of calculated rationality and wild illogicality, and he reacted to individuals and to whole social categories with what was excessive suspiciousness by most standards. He had a paranoiac streak. But most of the time he did not seem insane to those close to him.

2

*R. Service, **Stalin: A Biography**, 2005*

How much power did Stalin have?

Historians often debate the precise extent of Stalin's power. It is possible to argue that Stalin could not run everything personally and could not know everything that happened. Local party officials, especially in remoter regions of the USSR, sometimes acted independently of the centre. However, most historians accept that Stalin was the directing force, and even his closest colleagues were in awe or fear of him. When there was a significant change in policy, such as the decision to end the Great Terror or to sign the Non-Aggression Pact with Hitler in 1939, the initiative clearly came from Stalin. He did not often travel far from the Kremlin, but he was well informed through various party and personal channels about what was going on in the country. He took a personal interest when it suited him to: for example in signing thousands of death warrants during the purges. The Politburo, the policy-making group of leading Communists created by Lenin, met less and less frequently. Stalin preferred to work through individuals. The huge bureaucracy ran the USSR not because it was particularly efficient but because it was unchallenged and all-powerful. The administrators who ran the bureaucracy were not elected. They were selected by their political masters from a list, later known as the **Nomenklatura**, which consisted of people regarded as politically reliable.

Fig. 6 *Soviet propaganda poster: The working class breaking the chains of world Capitalism*

The bureaucracy was like a pyramid: the further up the pyramid, the fewer the party functionaries, and the more initiative they were allowed, until one reached the single leader at the top. Lenin had warned about the dangers of government getting into the hands of bureaucrats who became more concerned with protecting their own positions than running the country well, although he did little to stop this process which was already established by his death and then taken to a new level by Stalin. The results were described by a Russian critic of Stalin (Source 3):

> Symptoms of arrogance, conceit, intolerance of criticism, and susceptibility to flattery began to appear among some who previously had seemed to be modest and reliable revolutionaries... It was not the struggle with the [tsarist] autocracy, not jail or exile, that was the real test for revolutionaries. Much harder was the test of power, having the vast and powerful resources of the state at one's disposal... Bolshevik leaders... did acquire the habit of commanding, of administration by fiat [order], ignoring the opinion of the masses. Cut off from the people, they lost the ability to criticise Stalin's behaviour and the cult of his personality; on the contrary, they became increasingly dependent on him. Their change in life-style aroused dissatisfaction among workers and rank-and-file party members. One result was the relative ease with which Stalin subsequently destroyed such people, for he could picture their fall as the result not only of a struggle against 'spies' and 'wreckers' but also of the proletariat's struggle against corrupt and degenerate bureaucrats, a struggle to purge the party of petty bourgeois elements.

3   *R. Mevedev, **Let History Judge**, 1989*

Activity

Talking point

In groups, discuss: How far Stalin's regime was a personal dictatorship.

Activity

Challenge your thinking

A stretch and challenge topic for those who have previously studied Lenin: 'How far was Stalinism only a continuation of Leninism?'

■ The Communist Party and Soviet government

Government and party structures

The party was the main instrument through which Stalin exercised his dictatorship. Its organisation parallelled the Soviet government. The government structure (based on the 1936 Constitution) was as follows:

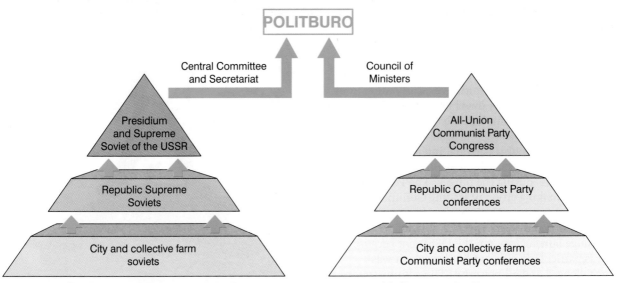

Fig. 7 *Political structure of the USSR*

Both Soviets elected a Presidium, whose president was Head of State. Below the Soviets was a pyramid of elected provincial, city, local and district Soviets. These provided local representation and put policies into practice at local level. In the later 1920s, only party members could be elected to Soviets. The All-Union Supreme Soviet met once or twice a year, elected by city and provincial Soviets. In reality, the Supreme Soviet was little more than a rubber stamp, approving laws drafted by the Secretariat of the Communist Party.

Democratic centralism

Elections to Soviets after 1936 were by secret ballot for all citizens over 18, except those in prison or insane. Before 1936, members of so-called 'bourgeois' classes such as kulaks were also excluded. Usually those elected were Communists, because the candidates had to come from a list approved by the party. People were strongly encouraged to vote as a patriotic duty, so the turnout at elections was usually about 99 per cent. Elections were regarded more as a vote of support for what the party and government were doing, rather than an opportunity for voters to choose alternative candidates.

This system was not democratic in a Western liberal sense. Stalin dismissed foreign criticism of Soviet democracy on the grounds that elections in capitalist countries were not really fair and open, because they 'took place in an atmosphere of class conflict and intimidation', whereas he claimed that Soviet political practice was based on 'mutual collaboration', and was 'the only thoroughly democratic constitution in the world'. The Soviet system was described as **democratic centralism**. People's views were passed up through the Soviets – this was the 'democratic' part. Decisions made at the top were then passed down to the people – this was the 'centralist' part.

Key term

Democratic centralism: a Leninist principle meaning that although all decision making was centralised in the party, it was a democratic process, since all party members were allowed their say, and the party had the interests of the whole socialist society at heart.

The party

The party was clearly the key institution. Those wishing to join the party were recommended by existing members, then underwent a trial period. Less than 10 per cent of the population joined the party. Joining opened up possibilities, and also privileges if one reached a higher level. Joining the party had clear advantages if one wanted to 'get on', and therefore many careerists obviously joined out of ambition rather than ideological commitment. However, joining the party also carried responsibilities, such as organising party meetings in the workplace. It could also be dangerous: being a party member in the 1930s made one more likely to be purged than any other group. The rapid growth in the party, from 1.25 million members in 1928 to 3.5 million by 1933 created its own problems: were all these new members reliable? The leaders spent much of the next few years either purging the party or trying to educate it better into the 'correct' political views. However, the party remained much more loosely organised and indeed chaotic than is the picture often created, and it is possible that the glorification of Stalin was partly an attempt to gloss over this fact. Stalin himself increasingly relied upon personal contacts and his personal secretariat to implement his policies, rather than using the official party administrative machine, which could be obstructive, as much through sheer inefficiency than deliberate intent.

Given that the party was clearly in control of policy and everyday life, and Stalin was firmly in control of the party, especially after 1934, it is fair to classify Stalin as a dictator.

Stalin gave a clear justification for the USSR being a one-party State (Source 4):

> A party is a part of a class, its most advanced part. Several parties, and consequently, freedom for parties, can exist only in a society in which there are antagonistic classes whose interests are mutually hostile and irreconcilable – in which there are, say, capitalists and workers, landlords and peasants, kulaks and poor peasants, etc. But in the USSR there are no longer such classes... In the USSR there are only two classes, workers and peasants, whose interests – far from being mutually hostile – are, on the contrary, friendly. Hence there is no ground in the USSR for the existence of several parties... In the USSR only one party can exist, the Communist Party, which courageously defends the interests of the workers and peasants to the very end.

4 *From a speech by Stalin in the mid-1930s*

The 1936 Constitution

Stalin issued a new constitution in 1936 to mark progress towards Socialism and to celebrate what he saw as the triumphs of the previous years. The constitution declared that Socialism had been achieved. It recognised only three classes – workers, peasants and the 'working intelligentsia'. Various civil rights were guaranteed, including freedom of the press and religion. Citizens were expected to work and were guaranteed the right to work, education and social welfare. The constitution provided for elections to directly involve all citizens and not just be dominated by representatives from party branches. The republics were given some rights of jurisdiction in their own areas, including primary education. However, in practice, there was no decentralisation

 Activity

Talking point

1. Why was the Communist Party more important than the State?

2. Did Stalin's system of government have any elements of democracy?

Activity

Source analysis

Read Source 4. How convincing was Stalin's argument for a one-party State?

Fig. 8 *Stalin steers the ship of the Communist State*

and the security services or government could override virtually anything. Therefore the constitution was largely a paper exercise, although it was in force until 1977. The main features of the personal dictatorship were firmly in place:

■ A cult of personality.

■ An emphasis on the all-important role of the leader.

■ Control over the population and the organs of government exercised by one party, in a very centralised system.

■ The use of terror and propaganda to reinforce control.

■ The ability to ignore any paper guarantees of individual rights.

This form of government characterised the USSR for most of the rest of its existence.

■ The impact of Stalinism

The command economy

As already seen in Chapter 4, the command economy was firmly in place soon after Stalin acquired power at the end of the 1920s. Its main features were centralised planning and target setting; an emphasis on heavy industry and defence; comparative neglect of agriculture, given a secondary role to industry; relative neglect of consumer goods; a greater emphasis on quantity and meeting targets than on quality; an economy driven by the State determining priorities rather than responding to consumer need. These features, embodied in the Five Year Plans, were to be the bedrock of the Soviet economy until the 1980s, even though the economy became steadily less successful in later years.

The politicisation of life

Marxists had always taken the view that it was difficult to separate politics from other areas of human activity. Political structures reflected the concerns of the dominant class in society. Stalin claimed that class differences had largely disappeared by the 1930s, and the only classes left (workers, peasants and intelligentsia) were in alliance with each other, with their interests looked after by the party. Therefore there was no need for independent organisations or pressure groups. Anybody who wanted to 'opt out' of the collectivist approach must be either insane or be a traitor bent on undermining the world's first worker's State. Stalinism went much further than NEP Russia in ensuring that all activity – be it artistic, sporting, intellectual, or whatever – served the interest of the people and State as a whole. All activity was politicised and had a message, as evident in movements like Socialist Realism.

Never have our fertile fields such a harvest shown,

Never have our villages such contentment known.

Never life has been so fair, spirits been so high,

Never to the present day grew so green the rye.

O'er the earth the rising sun sheds a warmer light,

Since it looked on Stalin's face it has grown more bright.

I am singing to my baby sleeping in my arms,

Grow like flowers in the meadow free from all alarm.

On your lips the name of Stalin will protect from harm,

You will learn the source of sunshine bathing all our land.

You will copy Stalin's portrait with your tiny hand.

5   *An Ode to Stalin on his 60th birthday (1939)*

> **Activity**
>
> **Source analysis**
>
> What does Source 5 suggest about the nature of Stalinist propaganda?

> **Activity**
>
> Try to listen to some music by Prokoviev and find out about other musicians who were active at this time, such as Shostakovich. What sort of music did Stalin find acceptable and why?

Social structure

In theory, all were equal in the worker's State. In practice, this was far from the case. Higher party functionaries, along with successful and conforming artists, were given great privileges in terms of wealth, access to housing and special goods. Ordinary people had minimal rights: for example, workers did not have free trade unions to represent their interests; peasants' movements were restricted by the passport system; most women were second-class citizens; certain groups such as priests suffered harsh discrimination. Skilled workers earned considerably more than unskilled workers. Because there were no independent organisations or media outlets to publicise perceived injustices, inequality was firmly built into Stalinism – except it was not called exploitation, but justified as 'socialist accumulation' by those who benefited.

Culture

As described on pages 117–20, cultural activity was closely controlled by the State. It was part of the politicisation of life. Censorship and the extensive use of propaganda were part of everyday existence and affected literature, art, the cinema, education and all means of communication.

'Revolutionary conservatism'

There was a major paradox in Stalinism. Leninism had been a revolutionary creed, overturning old institutions and old ideas, with a Utopian (idealistic) vision of the future. Stalinism continued to have some revolutionary features: especially the 'second revolution' in the

Fig. 9 *Satirical cartoon by Schilling against Stalin. 30th anniversary of the Soviet State. The Comintern leader (left); the Head of State (middle); the leaders of the Communist Party (right)*

countryside and towns which ended the NEP. This was a bold experiment. It was supposed to lead the USSR (and eventually other countries) into Socialism, and then as the socialist State became stronger and its enemies were overcome, the stage would be set for a transition to Communism. Under Communism the State would wither away, because the State was ultimately a repressive institution and would be unneccessary once class differences had disappeared and all people lived and worked in harmony.

Ironically, under Stalin the power of the State strengthened and showed no signs of even beginning to wither away. Stalin's argument in the 1930s was that as the USSR travelled on the path to Communism, so its enemies would become more desperate in their attempts to destroy it. Therefore it was right to strengthen the State, because it was necessary to protect the working class and the gains of the revolution. The State was to remain even under Communism, said Stalin, until the defeat of international Capitalism.

As enemies of Stalin such as Trotsky pointed out, the result was a huge bureaucracy, and in Stalin's USSR, it was a very brutal one. Maintaining the party and the bureaucracy almost seemed to become an end in itself. Those who ran the bureaucracy enjoyed great privileges and became reluctant to implement any changes that might change their status or even remove their reason for existing. Under Stalinism, it seemed that people were there to serve the bureaucracy rather than the other way round. The bureaucracy became more and more conservative. Nobody dared to challenge Stalin.

Even after Stalin's death, those politicians who recognised the need for some changes, for example to make the economy more efficient or the party more responsive to popular need, found that their efforts were undermined by apathy and self-interest, and above all, by bureaucratic obstructionism. Khrushchev, Stalin's successor, was driven out of the leadership partly because he did threaten to shake up the bureaucracy, so it turned on him. It was largely Stalin who had created this system or allowed it to develop.

The move to a more conservative approach was evident early on in Stalin's regime. The policy of class discrimination was ended in June 1931, when Stalin announced that old 'bourgeois' engineers would be rehabilitated, in order to help the economy. The policy of promoting people from the working class because they were 'proletarians' was replaced by an emphasis on ability and specialist skill, with accompanying material rewards. As described on pages 118–125, policy towards education, women and the family became more conservative. Stalinism seemed to be more about consolidation than change.

Stalin's personal contribution: a religion of national development

Many historians have argued that some of the characteristics of the USSR described above were not due just to Stalin, but already existed to some extent in the Russia of Lenin. They argue that Stalin simply took these characteristics to a new level. However, it is possible also to identify some features that were distinctly 'Stalinist':

One was a strong emphasis on Nationalism and patriotism. This was a new development. The early Bolsheviks had been quite international in outlook. They were educated men, who despised Russian backwardness, spent considerable time abroad in exile, and were quite cosmopolitan in attitude. They also believed in Marxism, which was an international creed, and looked to a future world order when the whole developed world would be socialist or communist, all men would be brothers and international boundaries would become unimportant. Stalin was not cosmopolitan. Although well educated, he was Georgian, spent most of his life in Georgia or Russia, and had limited experience of the outside world. He was less interested in foreign comrades, unless they served the interests of the USSR.

Stalin also faced an unexpected situation that Lenin had begun to experience before he died: the revolution had been consolidated in Russia alone. It did not spark a workers' revolution across Europe. Therefore the new Soviet State faced a hostile world, which tried to strangle Bolshevism at its birth. Fear of foreign intervention remained strong, especially in the 1930s when Nazism, with its strong anti-communist philosophy, took hold in Germany. It made sense to Stalin and others to concentrate on building the USSR's strength before considering the international advance of Communism.

Because of this, Stalinism developed early on a strong emphasis on Nationalism and patriotism. Building Soviet strength seemed as much about beating the enemy and creating national pride as about building Socialism. Stalin increasingly talked like an old-fashioned Russian nationalist, and Stalinism placed a high emphasis on cutting Russia off from foreign contacts and influences, unless they directly served Soviet interests, for example in foreign trade. This version of patriotism was to serve the USSR well in the coming war against Germany.

The sense of competition between the USSR and the outside world was also demonstrated in the cult of the hero which became very fashionable in the 1930s. The exploits of polar explorers, aviators and border guards were celebrated as national events, and the USSR tried to take credit for many scientific and technical advances, sometimes legitimately, sometimes not. To some extent, this drive for recognition was an attempt to show the superiority of Socialism, but it was also bound up with pride in the nation.

Learning outcomes

Through your study of this section you should have a good understanding of why propaganda was such an important part of Stalinism in the 1930s USSR. You should also understand what Stalinism actually was, and how Stalin's policies impacted upon different areas such as culture, ideology, society and on specific regions of the USSR.

When you have read the other chapters in this book, you should also be in a position to analyse what the strengths and weaknesses of the USSR were in 1941, after more than 10 years of Stalinist rule.

AQA Examination-style questions

(a) Explain why Stalin felt threatened by foreign powers before 1941. *(12 marks)*

  Part a) requires an awareness of why Stalin felt threatened both by Nazi Germany and the capitalist Western democracies, and possibly Japan too. You should produce a range of reasons and show the links between them.

(b) 'By 1941, Stalin had succeeded in ensuring that the USSR was in a much stronger position to defend itself against foreign attack than when he came to power.' Explain why you agree or disagree with this view. *(24 marks)*

  Part b) makes a typically firm statement and invites the student to agree or disagree with it. There is no right or wrong answer. You will probably decide that in many respects the USSR was in a stronger position than in 1929, if only for economic developments. However, the trick is to decide how much stronger, and to write a balanced answer that considers other aspects such as the terror, as well as analysing the economic impact of Stalin's policies. As in any essay answer, you must reach some sort of judgement and support it with plenty of evidence to get a high mark.

Conclusion

The USSR in 1941

Chapter 10 provided an overview of the strengths and weaknesses of the USSR on the eve of war against Germany. This conclusion will seek to summarise the impact of Stalin in the context of Soviet history between the 1920s and 1941.

Stalin as the heir of Lenin

Fig. 1 *Stalin at the 6th Party Congress of the Russian Communist Party*

Lenin's positive reputation, certainly within the USSR, lasted much longer after his death than Stalin's. Lenin was credited with great achievements, including of course the revolution itself. Whilst it is universally accepted that Stalin had a great impact on the USSR, many inside and outside the USSR maintained after Stalin's death that rather than continue Lenin's work, Stalin somehow undermined it, turning the USSR into a perversion of what was intended as the first workers' State.

This has always been too simple an explanation. Lenin was a ruthless leader. Whilst there were many apologists for the excesses under Lenin, such as the Red Terror after the revolution, they were more easily excused as a response to the desperate situation in which Russia found itself, trying to maintain its survival in the face of internal and external enemies. Stalin's excesses, such as the purges, seemed avoidable and far less excusable. This intepretation is now less easy to sustain. Historians have more evidence than before. We know, for example, that Lenin was just as capable of signing death warrants with as little thought as Stalin did. We do not know whether the USSR would have developed differently had Lenin lived longer or had he been succeeded by someone else such as Trotsky.

Fig. 2 *17th Party Congress of the Communist Party: 'Long live invincible Lenin's party' and 'Long live the great leader of the World Proletarian Revolution, comrade Stalin'*

Tables 1–5 show the ways in which Stalin changed the USSR from the condition in which Lenin had left it in 1924:

Table 1 *The Communist Party*

1924	1941
The party had a monopoly of power. All other parties had been banned, so there was no party democracy, although the Politburo still met and it was possible for leading Bolsheviks to debate policy.	The party was even more in control, and was much larger. Party organisation had no real independence and Stalin was firmly in control, often by-passing party organs altogether. Most Old Bolsheviks were gone and the new generation owed everything to Stalin.
On Lenin's death there was no clear leader.	

Table 2 *The bureaucracy*

This was already in place, and Lenin had been warning against it as something that would stifle progress.	The bureaucracy was well-established, much larger and more privileged than before. It was partly self-perpetuating and becoming resistant to change.
The USSR was already a one-party bureaucratic State.	

Table 3 *The economy*

In 1924, the USSR had a mixed economy. Heavy industry was State-owned, but smaller industries were privately owned, as were most farms. The USSR was still predominantly agriculturally based.	In 1941, almost all industry was nationalised and working to a central plan. The emphasis was on heavy industry. The USSR was an industrial power. Agriculture was collectivised or State-owned.

Table 4 *Terror*

Lenin had used terror against real of potential enemies without hesitation. He had instituted the secret police with arbitrary powers.	Terror was an integral part of Stalinism, although the Great Terror had been relaxed by 1941. The main difference from 1924 was that by now terror was more arbitrary and on a much larger scale.

Table 5 *Culture and society*

In 1924, the party had not fully imposed itself on society. Although there was censorship and propaganda, there was still an opportunity to experiment in the arts, and the party had limited control in some areas, especially rural ones.	In 1941, there were strong elements of totalitarianism in that all aspects of culture and society were closely controlled by the State, and there was little opportunity for independent thought or action.

Stalin used methods established by Lenin – especially the setting up of internal security services and the emphasis on class warfare – but took them to much greater extremes. His terror was on a much greater scale. His hold on the party was achieved by fear and terror, whereas Lenin's hold had depended much more on his personal reputation. Stalin adapted his policies to what he perceived were the needs of the time, although, like Lenin, he was always ready to come up with an ideological justification for those policies.

Fig. 3 *Propagandist parade in Red Square, Moscow*

We do not know how Lenin would have reacted to circumstances had he lived longer, and therefore to some extent the argument as to whether Stalin was the true heir of Lenin, or whether indeed he was a Marxist at all, can easily become a sterile debate. Stalin had followed Lenin whilst Lenin was alive, and in many respects simply consolidated or extended what Lenin had begun, for example in strengthening the role of the party. But Stalin had to develop his own policies. Historians are fond of declaring that it is unlikely that Lenin would have carried out the Five Year Plans in the way that Stalin did – but then as a socialist, presumably Lenin would have had to eventually implement a programme of industrialisation, and we have no way of knowing what methods he would have used, how it would have turned out and what disruption and suffering it might have caused.

Some of the features of Stalin's rule were not that dissimilar to the methods of the Tsar, although his authoritarianism was on a much more brutal scale than that of the recent tsars, partly because he devoted more resources to keeping both himself in power and the USSR on an accelerated road to socialist construction.

Stalin made few theoretical contributions to Marxist theory after 1929, except possibly his ideas on the role of the State in a socialist but pre-Communist society. Basically he was continuing and extending Leninism, with a particular focus on the revolution in order to carry out profound economic and social change. At the same time, the nature of the international situation that Stalin's USSR found itself in, and one not foreseen by his predecessors, led Stalin to increasingly fuse Russian Nationalism with Soviet Socialism and focus on policies such as self-sufficiency.

Stalin did what most successful politicians do: he combined theory with pragmatism, that is, adapting to circumstances. He has remained a controversial figure both inside and outside Russia because he carried out this fusion in a particularly authoritarian and often brutal way that has evoked emotions such as horror and hatred. But it has also commanded a strong tinge of respect amongst those, particularly older citizens in his homeland, who remembered the certainties and the comfort of having a 'strong' leader who 'won the war'. Stalin was remembered not just as a tyrant, responsible for more deaths than any other contemporary, but as the man who successfully led the USSR through a series of crises, some self-inflicted and some forced on the country by its enemies.

Glossary

A

anarchism: a belief in a political system without an organised government.

apparat: the bureaucracy or party machine that controlled all aspects of Soviet life.

apparatchik: slang term for government or party official.

Armenia: a Soviet republic.

Azerbaijan: a Soviet republic.

B

Baltic States: Estonia, Latvia, Lithuania: three republics independent from 1917, but annexed by the USSR in 1940.

Belorussia: a Soviet republic.

Bolshevik: the so-called majority faction of the Social Democrat Party, and led by Lenin.

C

Central Committee: party organisation responsible for carrying out decisions of Party Congresses.

collectivisation: the amalgamation of privately-owned farms into larger collective units.

commissar: a head of a government department ('minister').

Congress: party meeting, held irregularly either yearly or at longer intervals, which discussed party issues.

F

Five Year Plans: the system by which the Soviet economy was planned and run after 1928.

G

General Secretary: the official leader of the Communist Party.

Georgia: a Soviet republic, home of Stalin.

Glavit: the Soviet Censorship Office, set up in 1922.

Gosplan: the State Planning Commission (founded in 1921), producing the Five Year Plans.

GPU/OGPU: the Soviet political police, 1922–34.

Gulag: the system of labour camps.

I

intelligentsia: the class of people, distinct from peasants or workers, and relying on mental work or talents.

K

Kazakhstan: a Soviet republic.

Kirghizstan: a Soviet republic.

kolkhoz: a collective farm.

Komsomol: the Communist Party youth organisation.

Kremlin: the Soviet seat of government, in Moscow, from 1918.

kulak: a wealthy peasant.

L

Left Opposition: group associated with Trotsky, Zinoviev and Kamenev and opposed to Stalin in the mid-1920s.

M

Marxism-Leninism: the official ideology of the USSR.

Menshevik: the non-Leninist wing of the Social Democratic Party, destroyed in the years after the revolution.

Moldavia: a Soviet republic.

MTS: Machine Tractor Station, which hired tractors and other machinery to collective farms.

N

NEP: the New Economic Policy, the economic system in the USSR between 1921 and 1928.

Nepman: someone who profited from the NEP.

NKVD: the Soviet political police, 1934–43.

Nomenklatura: the list of important posts in the party and State from which postholders were chosen.

O

Orgburo: the body focusing on party organisation.

Orthodox Church: the most important church in the USSR, formerly the official or Established Church.

P

permanent revolution: Trotsky's theory that the party should focus on ensuring successful socialist revolutions worldwide.

Politburo: small, decision-making policy of the party, less important under Stalin.

Pravda: the leading Soviet newspaper.

proletariat: the industrial working class.

purges: the 'cleansing' of the party or elements of the population at large, involving dismissal, arrest, prison or death, usually for crimes deemed 'political'.

R

Rabkrin: the Workers' and Peasants' Inspectorate, which monitored the bureaucracy, 1920–34.

Red Army: the Soviet Army, formed in 1918.

Right Opposition: group led by Bukharin, favouring moderate treatment of the peasantry, and defeated by Stalin in 1929.

S

Secretariat: the body that ensured party decisions were carried out.

Show Trials: public staged trials at which 'enemies' of the regime confessed their guilt.

Socialism in One Country: the policy, associated with Stalin, that the USSR should concentrate on building Socialism at home before world revolution.

Socialist Realism: the officially approved art form in the 1930s, making all art forms part of Stalinist propaganda.

Soviet: the Russian word for 'council'.

Soviet of Nationalities: one of the chambers of the Supreme Soviet.

Soviet of the Union: one of the chambers of the Supreme Soviet, elected by republican Soviets.

sovkhoz: a State-owned farm.

Sovnarkom: the official government, or Council of People's Commissars.

Stakhanovites: shock workers who achieved high levels of labour productivity.

T

Tajikstan: a Soviet republic.

Turkestan: a Soviet republic.

U

Ukraine: a Soviet republic.

Uzbekistan: a Soviet republic.

V

VSNKh: the Supreme Council of the National Economy, which managed industry 1917–34.

Y

Yezhovshchina: name often given to the Great Terror or purges of the mid-1930s.

Bibliography

General accounts

Useful outline in the 'Teach Yourself' series:
Evans, D. (2005) *Stalin's Russia*, Hodder Headline.

Concise overview:
Gill, G. (1990) *Stalinism*, Macmillan.

A concise, useful analysis of the main themes:
Grant, J. (1998) *Stalin and the Soviet Union*, Longman.

Concise and readable narratives and analyses:
Lee, S. (1999) *Stalin and the Soviet Union*, Routledge.

A solid account covering the main themes:
Mawdsley, E. (1998) *The Stalin Years*, Manchester University Press.

Useful analyses, chronologies, glossaries, etc:
McCauley, M. (1997) *Russia 1917–1941*, Sempringham Studies.

Useful on analysis and interpretations:
Ward, C. (1993) *Stalin's Russia*, Edward Arnold.

Biographies

Very detailed but highly readable biographies:
Sebag Montefiore, S. (2004) *Stalin: At the Court of the Red Tsar* and (2007) *The Young Stalin*, Phoenix.

A detailed, thoughtful biography:
Service, R. (2005) *Stalin*, Pan Books.

Interesting Russian perspective:
Volkogonov, D. (1991) *Stalin: Triumph and Tragedy*, Prima Publishing.

Source books

A useful collection of sources:
Boobyer, P. (2000) *The Stalin Era*, Routledge.

Novels

Imaginative and detailed novel of the terror by a Russian author:
Rybakov, A. (1989) *Children of the Arbat*, Arrow Books.

More specialised studies: mainly for teachers

Detailed on all aspects of the camp system:
Applebaum, A. (2003) *Gulag: A History*, Penguin.

Focuses on NEP Russia, very useful:
Brovkin, V. (1998) *Russia After Lenin*, Routledge.

Detailed and authoritative on the economy:
Davies, R., Harrison, M. and Wheatcroft, S. (1994) *The Economic Transformation of the Soviet Union 1913–1945*, Cambridge University Press.

Useful on social history:
Fitzpatrick, S. (2000) *Everyday Stalinism*, Oxford University Press.

Detailed on the workings of the terror:
Rayfield, D. (2005) *Stalin and his Hangmen*, Penguin.

A detailed analysis of the impact of the terror:
Thurston, R. (1996) *Life and Terror in Stalin's Russia 1934–1941*, Yale University Press.

Acknowledgements

The author and publisher would like to thank the following for permission to reproduce material:

Source texts:

p10, Vera Inber (1924) 'Five days and nights'. Taken from Yakovlev, B. V. (1980) *Lenin in Soviet Poetry*, Progress Publishers; p19, Segal, R. (1983) *The Tragedy of Leon Trotsky*, Penguin; p19, Volkogonov, D. (1996) *Trotsky: The Eternal Revolutionary*, HarperCollins; p32, Quoted in Brovkin, V. (1998) *Russia After Lenin*, Routledge; p33, Quoted from Victor Serge, 'Vignettes of NEP' in Brovkin, V. (1998) *Russia After Lenin*, Routledge; p33, Quoted in Brovkin, V. (1998) *Russia After Lenin*, Routledge; p38, Quoted in Evans, D. (2005) *Stalin's Russia*, Hodder Headline; p40, Quoted in Brovkin, V. (1998) *Russia After Lenin*, Routledge; p43, Kukushkin, Y. (1981) *History of the USSR*, Progress Publishers; p43, Davies, R., Harrison, M. and Wheatcroft, S. (eds.) (1994) *The Economic Transformation of the Soviet Union, 1913–1945*, Cambridge University Press; p48, Quoted in Kuromiya, H. (1990) *Stalin's Industrial Revolution*, Cambridge University Press; p48, Adapted from a speech in Kuromiya, H. (1990) *Stalin's Industrial Revolution*, Cambridge University Press; p49, Quoted in Kuromiya, H. (1990) *Stalin's Industrial Revolution*, Cambridge Univeristy Press; p49, Quoted in Boobbyer, P. (2000) *The Stalin Era*, Routledge; p50, Adapted from (1981) *A Dictionary of Political Economy*, Progress Publishers; p51, From Golubeva, T. and Gellerstein, L. (1976) *Early Russia – the USSR*, Novosti Publishing House; p55, Nove, A. (1969) *An Economic History of the USSR*, Penguin; p62, Kukushkin, Y. (1981) *History of the USSR*, Progress Publishers; p64, Quoted in Evans, D. (2005) *Stalin's Russia*, Hodder Headline; p68, Quoted in Sakwa, R. (1999) *The Rise and Fall of the Soviet Union*, Routledge; p69, Quoted in Catchpole, B. (1974) *A Map History of Russia*, Heinemann; p69, Quoted in Reiman, M. (1987) *The Birth of Stalinism*, IB Tauris; p69, Quoted in Stacey, F. (1970) *Stalin and the Making of Modern Russia*, Edward Arnold; p69, Quoted in Stacey, F. (1970) *Stalin and the Making of Modern Russia*, Edward Arnold; p71, From Serge, V. (1973) *From Lenin to Stalin*, Anchor Foundation; p71, From Serge, V. (1973) *From Lenin to Stalin*, Anchor Foundation; p78, Brovkin, V. (1998) *Russia After Lenin*, Routledge; p80–81 Adapted from Thurston, R. (1996) *Life and Terror in Stalin's Russia 1934–1941*, Yale University Press; p81 Adapted from Volkogonov, D. (1988) *Stalin: Triumph and Tragedy*, Prima Publishing; p81 Adapted from Kopolev, L. (1981) 'The Education of a True Believer' quoted in Boobbyer, P. (2000) *The Stalin Era*, Routledge; p83, Bukharin, letter of an Old Bolshevik (1938); p89, Quoted in Boobyer, P. (2000) *The Stalin Era*, Routledge; p89, Adapted from 'Molotov Remembers', 1993. Quoted in Boobbyer, P. (2000) *The Stalin Era*, Routledge; p89, Taken from Nadezhda Mandelstam's memoirs. Published in 1975 in *Hope Against Hope*, Penguin; p89, Adapted from a speech by Andrei Vishinsky (1938), chief prosecutor in the Show Trials. Quoted in Sakwa, R. (1999) *The Rise and Fall of the Soviet Union*, Routledge; p92, Quoted in Evans, D. (2005) *Stalin's Russia*, Hodder Headline; p93, Quoted in von Geldern, J. and Stites, R. (1995) *Mass Culture in Soviet Russia*, Indiana University Press; p96, Published in *Pravda*, December 1937. Quoted in van Geldern, R. and Stites, R. (1995) *Mass Culture in Soviet Russia*, Indiana University Press; p98, Adapted from Rybakov, A. (1989) *Children of the Arbat*, Arrow Books; p98, Adapted from Ward, C. (1993) *Stalin's Russia*, Edward Arnold; p105, Scott, J. (1973) *Behind the Urals: An American Worker in Russia's City of Steel*, Indiana University Press; p105, From the poem sequence *Requiem*; p106, Applebaum, A. (2003) *Gulag: A History*, Penguin; p106, Applebaum, A. (2003) *Gulag: A History*, Penguin; p111, Adapted from Lynch, M. (2001) *Stalin and Khrushchev: The USSR 1924–64*, Hodder; p111, Adapted from Fainsod, M. (1989) *Smolensk Under Soviet Rule*, Unwin Hyman; p111, Adapted from McCauley, M. (1997) *Russia 1917–1941*, Sempringham Studies; p122, Quoted in Brovkin, V. (1998) *Russia After Lenin*, Routledge; p134, Service, R. (2005) *Stalin: A Biography*, Pan Books; p135, Mevedev, R. (1989) 'Let History Judge', quoted in Daniels, R. (ed.) (1990) *The Stalin Revolution*, Heath & Co; p139, Quoted in Stacey, F. (1970) *Stalin and the Making of Modern Russia*, Edward Arnold

Bibliothèque nationale/Snark archives/Phtos12.com – Oasis 140; John Laver 17 (right), 41, 53, 56 (top), 69, 79, 83, 87 (bottom), 88, 97 (top), 97 (bottom), 123 (left), 123 (right), 124, 125, 126, 135; Edimedia Art Archive 10, 12, 23 (bottom), 30, 39, 40 (top), 46, 115, 121, 122, 132, 138; Photos12.com 28; Photos12.com – Bertelsmann Lexikon 56 (bottom), 78, 93, 131; Photos12.com – JSR/DR 101, 116; Photos12.com – Oasis 17 (left), 18, 22, 23 (top), 27, 32, 40 (bottom), 45, 54, 55, 58, 63 (bottom), 63 (top), 64 (top), 66, 70, 74, 75, 76, 99, 100, 102, 113, 127, 143, 144; RIA Novosti/Topfoto 72; Topfoto – Roger Viollet 89; Topfoto 60, 61, 64 (bottom), 85, 87 (top), 91, 96, 104, 109, 119, 134 (bottom), 146; Topham Picturepoint 15, 20; World History Archive 11, 14, 16, 34, 118, 134 (top)

Cover photograph: courtesy of Corbis/Reuters

Grateful thanks are offered to Valery-Anne Giscard d'Estaing, Dora Swick, Ann Asquith and Samuel Manning for assistance with the Photo Research for this project.

Photo Research by Unique Dimension Ltd.
www.uniquedimension.com

Index